MEMOIR

OF

THOMAS HARDY,

FOUNDER OF, AND SECRETARY TO,

THE

LONDON CORRESPONDING SOCIETY,

FOR

DIFFUSING USEFUL POLITICAL KNOWLEDGE

AMONG THE

PEOPLE OF GREAT BRITAIN & IRELAND,

AND FOR

PROMOTING PARLIAMENTARY REFORM,

From its Establishment, in Jan. 1792,

UNTIL HIS ARREST, ON A

FALSE CHARGE OF HIGH TREASON,

On the 12th of MAY, 1794.

WRITTEN BY HIMSELF.

He was a man, from vice and folly free—
No danger could his steady soul appal;
No slave to prejudice or passion, he
Esteem'd his fellow-men as brethren all.

Integrity his shield, and Truth his guide,
Unaw'd, he laboured in his Country's cause;
For that he liv'd, for that he would have died,
A Martyr to her liberty and laws;—
Firm to his purpose, virtuously severe,
He fear'd his God, but had no other fear.

D. MACPHERSON.

LONDON:

JAMES RIDGWAY, PICCADILLY.

M.DCCC.XXXII.

TO

SIR FRANCIS BURDETT, Bart. M.P.

THE FOLLOWING MEMOIR

IS

DEDICATED

BY

HIS GRATEFUL AND MUCH

OBLIGED SERVANT,

THOMAS HARDY.

ADVERTISEMENT.

The duty now devolves upon me, of informing the reader, that Mr. Hardy, having lived to see the last sheet of his Memoir from the press, breathed his last, about eight o'clock on the morning of Thursday, the 11th instant, at his apartments, 30, Queen's Row, Pimlico.

His extreme temperance, added to a strong and robust constitution, preserved him, through a long life, from many of those chronic disorders which, too often, embitter the lives of men of different habits. Some time before he retired from business, in 1815, his health suffered from the anxiety attending a losing concern, but, as soon as that was got rid of, he recovered, and, with the exception of slight rheumatic pains, occasionally, in his legs, he continued almost free from bodily ailments until last year, when, going to the city in a stiff-springed *omnibus*, he was so violently shook, that it brought on a stranguary, which, after much suffering, proved fatal to him.

From the beginning of the last severe attack, about three weeks ago, it became evident that he was approaching his end. Of this he himself was perfectly sensible, and his mind was prepared to meet it as became a man and a Christian.

In his person, Mr. Hardy was of fine proportions, near six feet high, before he began to stoop; large breasted, broad shouldered, and muscular, without the least inclination to corpulency. He was, indeed, such a man, in body and mind, as we may suppose the patriots to have been who followed those immortal heroes, an Alfred and a Wallace, in their attempts to give freedom to their respective countries.

In his manners he was mild, affable, and unassuming; and it may be safely affirmed, that he never made a personal enemy. The leading features of his character were moral courage, benevolence, and integrity, from the practice of which virtues no worldly consideration could deter him, if he saw any chance of being useful to his fellow creatures.

From vanity he was altogether free, his common saying being, that the greatest talents, exercised under the controul of the best judgment, and for the best purposes, did not give a man a right to be vain, for, that when a man did all the good in his power, he did no more than his duty. He, however, allowed that the praise of good men is desirable, forasmuch as it confirms our own approbation of our own best actions.

Ye vain, ye frivolous, ye prodigal, ye proud, behold this good man's mortal career, and learn to amend your lives, learn that man has not been created for himself alone, but for all mankind. Ye false patriots, think of him, blush, tremble, and reform. Ye true patriots, if a momentary temptation to waver should come across your minds, think of Thomas Hardy, and be firm.

Ye who are called noble by descent or creation, contemplate the life of this man, " who held the patent of his nobility immediately from Almighty God,"* and let your actions be suitable to your exalted ranks; learn that virtue is true nobility.

D. MACPHERSON.

October 16, 1832.

* Burns.

PREFACE.

THE greater part of the following Memoir was written upwards of thirty-four years ago. It was begun at the solicitation of some friends; but being too much engaged in business at that time to attend to it properly, I was obliged to lay it aside, and it remained in its hiding place until very lately.

The London Corresponding Society did more in the eight or nine years of its existence, to diffuse political knowledge among the people of Great Britain and Ireland than all that had ever been done before. Its Members *devoted* themselves to the cause of justice and humanity. They laboured zealously, intrepidly, and honestly, although they beheld the guilty arm of power suspended over their heads and ready to crush them, in order to promote the happiness of their fellow citizens.

A correct history of such a Society, the present generation,—who are likely to reap the fruits of its labours—cannot but highly appreciate; and I am happy to say that such a work is in the course of preparation, by a Gentleman every way well qualified for the task,—Mr. Francis Place, who has been upwards of twenty years collecting materials for it.

It is for that reason that many things are omitted in the following Memoir, which would otherwise find a place in it; but brief as these notices are, I earnestly hope they will excite the curiosity of the younger part of the present race to know something of the important Trials for *High Treason*, which took place near forty years ago, and the issue of which saved them from the most absolute and deplorable slavery being entailed upon them before they were born.

I have chosen to write in the third, rather than in the first person, merely, to obviate the necessity of calling the great *I* so repeatedly to my assistance; though I do not, by any means, consider that, what is called, egotism consists in the use, but in the manner of using, that letter.

THOMAS HARDY.

MEMOIR

OF

THOMAS HARDY.

As every man, whose actions, from whatever cause, have acquired publicity, is sure, in many things, to be misrepresented, such a man has an undoubted right, nay, it becomes his duty, to leave to posterity a true record of the real motives that influenced his conduct. The following Memoir, therefore, requires no apology, and none is offered.

Thomas Hardy* was born in the parish of Larbert,†

---

* The first of the name was a Frenchman, who was cup-bearer to John, King of France, and was taken prisoner along with that Monarch, by Edward the Black Prince, and brought to England. At an entertainment, the King of England desired his cup-bearer to fill a cup of wine to the worthiest in company, upon which he presented it to his own master. The cup-bearer to the King of France, taking this as an insult offered to his master, struck the English cup-bearer a blow on the ear, upon which the King of France called out *trop, trop, Hardie;* but the King of England exclaimed, *sera deshormais Hardie!* Upon this he took the name of Hardie; and the King of Scotland, who, at that time, was also prisoner in England, upon being set at liberty, carried him along with him to Scotland, and gave him the lands of Corregarff in Mar, where they flourished, until a quarrel happening with the Clan of Grant, the Hardies murdered the Chief of that Clan, and, in consequence, their estates were forfeited. They were followers of the family of Huntly.

Motto of the Hardies :—*Sera deshormais Hardie.*

† About a mile from the forest of Torwood, famous in Scottish history as the place where, in the hollow trunk of an extraordinary large oak tree, many of the exploits of that great man and true patriot, Sir William Wallace, were planned. The writer remembers having often visited

in Stirlingshire, in Scotland, on the 3rd day of March, 1752. His Grandfather, Walter Hardy, was an Officer in the Army, in what is called the German war, but with what rank the writer could not learn. Before he became a soldier he had a small estate, consisting of some houses, both in Edinburgh and Falkirk, which he mortgaged, and was never able to redeem.*

His Father, whose name was also Walter, was bred to a sea-faring life in the merchants' service. He married a respectable woman, whose relations were numerous and respectable, and for several years followed his profession with such diligence, that it was supposed when he died, on a homeward voyage from America, he left enough to enable his widow and three children to live comfortably in that cheap part of the country.

The death of Walter Hardy happened in 1760, when his eldest son, Thomas, was no more than eight years of age; and, unfortunately, as is too frequently the case, his affairs having got into bad hands, his widow found herself unable to give Thomas an education suitable to the clerical profession, according to the original intentions of her deceased husband and herself.

Her Father, Thomas Walker, a shoemaker by trade, on learning the hapless state of Mrs. Hardy's affairs, took Thomas under his own care and protection, and put him to school to learn reading, writing, and arithmetic. At

Wallace's tree, above sixty years ago; and he has learnt, with regret, that a Goth, into whose hands the estate fell, has since destroyed every vestige of it.

* His Grandson, Thomas, who was his legal heir, after he came of age, took some measures to recover them: with this view he had some communications with Mr. Livingston, the person on whom they devolved after the death of him who had advanced the money on them; but not being in circumstances to incur law expenses, he was obliged to give the matter up, although the first professional gentlemen, both in Stirling and Edinburgh, assured him that the case was quite clear.

that time the price of tuition was no more than a penny a week; before he left school it rose to three-halfpence, and now it is a shilling.

When he arrived at a proper age, his Grandfather taught him his own business. After having learnt as much as he could from his kind relative, he went to Glasgow, that beautiful and populous city, to improve himself in his trade. At that period the traffic between that city and America was very great, and many adventurers went and established manufactories of various kinds. One of these adventurers, a Mr. Ingram, who had projected a shoe factory at Norfolk, in Virginia, was returned, principally with a view of engaging workmen to go out with him.

He engaged many; and Thomas Hardy entered into an agreement with him to superintend the concern for five years. The terms were flattering; the agreement was signed on both sides, and they were to embark in a few days; but his relations interfered and prevented his going, urging that he could not legally enter into an agreement, being then under twenty-one years of age. Very soon after, the town of Norfolk was burnt to ashes, in one of the mad fits of the British Government, in the beginning of the American war. His first project being thus frustrated, he left Glasgow, and went to the iron works at Carron, where he followed the bricklaying business for some time. The Carron Company having just then established their manufactory for cast iron, were much in want of hands to carry on their buildings, and gave great encouragement to bricklayers. While here working with several others, on the second story of a large house that was being built for Mr. Roebuck, one of the proprietors, an accident happened that had nearly cost him his life; the scaffold gave way, and they were precipitated into the cellar, covered with boards, bricks, and mortar. One man was killed, and others much hurt: Hardy was carried home, much bruised; but with proper care he soon recovered, but returned no more to the bricklaying business.

He recommenced the trade of shoemaking with James Wilson, who had just settled in that part of the country from London; and having much conversation with his master about the metropolis, his curiosity was excited, and he determined to see it. With that view, he engaged a passage on board the Stirling, Carron smack, *Stewart Boyd* master, and, in eleven days, arrived in London, 23rd April, 1774, where he was a total stranger, with no more than eighteen-pence in his pocket: however, before that was expended, he found employment. He had a letter of introduction from his late master, to Mr. John Kerr, a most worthy character, with whom he lodged the first night, and with whom, and with his amiable family, he maintained afterwards the most friendly intercourse. The acquaintance of Mr. Kerr procured him that of others, of dispositions and turns of mind similar to his own. Hardy was, from his earliest years, of a sedate and serious turn of mind; avoiding all those scenes of dissipation, which, too often, lead astray the youthful and unwary, to the ruin of both their morals and their constitutions. It must, however, be owned, that a disposition to what is falsely called a life of pleasure, affords adventures, which, when afterwards related, conduce greatly to the entertainment of certain readers; but such as peruse these pages must expect nothing of the kind.

The life of a plain industrious citizen affords nothing of the light or the ludicrous circumstances which compose a great part of the frivolous reading of the present day.

Being of a contemplative and serious turn of mind, Hardy, soon after his settling in London, became acquainted with many of the middle and lower classes of

Dissenters: among these he had a number of highly respected and intimate friends, by whom he was much valued on account of his peaceable disposition and suavity of manners. He became, and continued many years, a member of the congregation which met in Crown Court, Russell Street, Covent Garden, under the ministry of Mr. Cruden. In 1784, some transactions, to which he was a party, took place in that congregation, and which may not be improper here briefly to relate. The Society was a numerous and highly respectable one, and paid their Pastor a considerable salary. At this period a vacancy occurred, by the death of Mr. Cruden, and candidates from various parts of England and Scotland, continued, for near two years, to preach in their turns with little approbation. One, however, at length appeared, who gave great satisfaction to the people, a Mr. James Chambers, from Scotland, a very eloquent and powerful preacher. Hardy, being zealously attached to the congregation, and having its interest much at heart, observed, with regret, that many of the members were leaving it, on account of its unsettled state. He, therefore, wrote privately to Mr. Chambers, to know if he would accept a call, if one were given him. Mr. Chambers replied by letter in the affirmative, provided the call was signed by a majority of the whole body. He communicated this circumstance to a friend; and they having consulted two or three others, again wrote to him, and again received a satisfactory reply. They then called a meeting of as many as they could inform of the business. The meeting was held in a large private room, and a greater number attended than was expected from so short a notice. Hardy was appointed chairman, and he opened the business by informing them, in a few words, the purpose for which they were called together. After a good deal of conversation, they adjourned, having appointed another meeting, which was still more numerously attended. At that meeting a deputation was appointed to wait upon the Elders or Managers, to request that they would call a general meeting of the Church, to consider the propriety of giving Mr. Chambers a call.

With this request the Elders refused to comply, alledging, or, at least, insinuating, that there was something wrong in his character; but what it was they would not satisfy the deputation. By the people, who very much esteemed Mr. Chambers, this was deemed calumny; and the consequence was, that the congregation became divided into two parties, the Elders, and their adherents on the one side, and the friends of Chambers, the greater number, on the other.

A correspondence was commenced immediately with many Ministers and others in Scotland, who knew Chambers, in order to learn if his moral character was good; and many certificates of his unblemished reputation were received.

In the mean time, the Elders were ransacking all quarters, in order to discover something to justify them in their objections, and to verify their insinuations: and they, at last, succeeded in discovering that he had two wives then living, one in Scotland, and another in England. Upon this, a meeting of both parties was thought requisite, and also to have Mr. Chambers present, that the affair might be publicly and properly discussed. The result was, that both sides became pretty well satisfied of the truth of what had been alledged against Chambers. Thus ended a controversy, which had been carried on smartly for nearly two years, and which had threatened the dissolution of the Society; the people contending that they had a right to the man of their choice, and the

Elders as strenuously resisting that right. This circumstance illustrates the saying, " how small a spark kindleth a great fire."

Another disagreeable circumstance happened one Sunday at the Chapel of the same congregation, of which Hardy was also the innocent cause. Happening to meet Lord George Gordon, with whom he was intimate, he asked his Lordship to come next Sunday, to hear a young man from the Highlands of Scotland, preach. Lord George said he would, and seemed even anxious to hear him; but it happened, through some accident or disappointment, that Mr. Bean, the gentleman of whom Hardy spoke, did not preach that day, but another in his place, who was not very acceptable to the congregation.

This man *read* his sermon in a monotonous manner, and without the least animation, which so displeased Lord George, that he interrupted him in the midst of his discourse, by telling him, that it was contrary to the rules of the Kirk of Scotland for the Minister to *read his sermon from the pulpit;* and this he proceeded to prove from the Confession of Faith, and Directory for public worship.

However lightly they might have thought of the preacher, so extraordinary an interruption gave great offence to many of the congregation, and much confusion consequently ensued. Lord George knew no person present, very few of them knew him, and, unfortunately, Hardy happened to be detained at home by the illness of one of his family. Lord George seeing none whom he knew, called loudly for Hardy, who had invited him there, and who he supposed had played him a trick; the congregation, on the other hand, thought that Hardy had sent Lord George to the meeting to create a disturbance, so that poor Hardy between them was in an awkward situation; yet it must be confessed, though he was perfectly ignorant and innocent of the whole affair, that the conclusion which each of the parties had drawn, though hasty, was not unreasonable.

Hardy, as already mentioned, was very intimate with Lord George Gordon, but was, by no means, an approver of any of his wild schemes: so far from it, that he often told him, with honest bluntness, both verbally and by letter, how much he differed from him in opinion on many subjects. Nevertheless, he always entertained, and expressed a sincere respect for the many virtues, and amiable qualities of that misguided, but much injured man; and was of opinion, that his life fell a sacrifice to the malice of his persecutors. Here, however, it may not, perhaps, be prudent to state who they were, whether ecclesiastical or political, or probably both.

At the period of his arrival in London, the American war was commenced, and then, as well as now, politics were the general topics of conversation in almost every company. His heart always glowed with the love of freedom, and was feelingly alive to the sufferings of his fellow creatures. He listened with attention to the arguments he heard advanced for and against the conduct of the Administration towards the Colonies; and as he was then unwilling to believe it as bad as it was represented by the partizans of the American people, he found himself frequently involved in disputes in their defence. In those disputes, however, he felt rather diffident of his own knowledge on the subject. This was the state of his mind with respect to the American war, until he met with and read Dr. Price's celebrated Treatise on Civil Liberty. The arguments brought forward in that masterly work, were, to him, so convincing, that he found himself compelled to adopt its principles. He saw that it was not only necessary for the happiness of the trans-atlantic patriots themselves, that the struggle should terminate in their favour; but that even the future happiness of the whole human race was concerned in the event. From that moment he became one of the warmest and most sincere advocates for the *right* cause.

In the year 1781, he married the youngest daughter of Mr. Priest, a carpenter and builder in Chesham, in Buckinghamshire, with whom he lived, in spite of all the tricks of fortune, in the most perfect state of connubial happiness. She bore him six children, who all died young—the last of them, still-born, found a grave with its hapless mother, who died on the 27th of August, 1794, in the unfortunate manner which shall be hereafter related. For many years after his marriage he followed his business with various success, and refused several advantageous offers which had been made to him if he would go to America; but he was strongly attached to his native country, and besides something always happened, in a manner to him unaccountable, to overthrow every momentary inclination of his own, and every effort of those who endeavoured to persuade him to emigrate.

In the latter end of the year 1791, a proposal was made to him, as it was pretended, very much calculated to advance his circumstances, to enter into a partnership with a currier and a leather cutter, who undertook, if he would engage in the manufactory of boots and shoes, to furnish leather, and to find a market for as many as he should make. To this proposal he agreed, and for that purpose took the house, *afterwards so well known*, No. 9, Piccadilly, and began with that active industry which nothing could ever depress, to fulfil his part of the contract he had entered into; when, lo! one of those instances of treachery, too common, but too little attended to, in corrupt and luxurious communities, threatened to overwhelm him and his family in utter ruin. Before he was well settled in the house he had engaged, his pretended friends deserted him, broke through the agreement they had made, sent in their bills at a short date, which, to avoid law expenses, he paid when due. The only excuse that can be offered for such conduct is, that their own affairs were not so prosperous as they expected. In this affair he experienced the great value of a good character; for having no capital of his own, he must, unavoidably, have given up business, had not unsolicited friendship come forward, with timely aid, which enabled him to carry on his trade until the memorable period at which he was arrested for High Treason, which circumstance shall be more particularly noticed presently.

However, notwithstanding every personal effort of his own, and the support of his friends, he soon began to feel the heavy pressure of the daily accumulating taxes, and the consequent rise in the prices of all the necessaries of life. He knew the country to be productive, and its inhabitants to be industrious and ingenious; therefore, the distress which he saw every where around him could not arise from the fault of the soil, or of those who occupied it, and the cause must be sought for somewhere else. It required no extraordinary penetration, once the enquiry was begun, to be able to trace it to the corrupt practices of men falsely calling themselves the representatives of the people, but who were, in fact, selected by a comparatively few influential individuals, who preferred their own particular aggrandisement to the general interest of the community.

The next enquiry naturally arose—Was the cause of the people hopeless? Must they and their posterity for ever groan under this intolerable load? Could not the nation, by a proper use of its moral powers, set itself free? Hardy thought it could; and he projected the plan of " the London Corresponding Society," as a means of informing the people of the violence that had been committed on their most sacred rights, and of uniting them in an endeavour to recover those rights. Why the Father of that Society remained unknown, except to two or three persons, until after the State Trials, is thus accounted for. He saw, with pleasure, that it was bidding fair to overturn a long established system of corruption and oppression, and he was afraid that it might operate to its prejudice were it made publicly known, that so obscure an individual was its founder. He saw his intentions to do good in the course of being fulfilled, and he never had any vanity to gratify. He was often asked who began the Society, but for the above reason he always evaded the question. Some said it was J. Horne Tooke; others, that it was Thomas Paine; but neither of them had any hand in it.

So prevalent, however, was the opinion, that the Attorney General, in his opening speech, on Hardy's trial, made use of the following words, which may be found in the report of that trial, taken in short hand by Mr. Ramsay, and published by Mr. Ridgway, page 57. "The London Corresponding Society was modelled by some of the leading Members, and owes its corporate existence, and was formed under the Constitutional Society." It has been already shewn that this must have been an error; for, in fact, the Constitutional Society had ceased its meetings for several years, and was not re-opened until three months after the London Corresponding Society had been modelled by Hardy, as above: and it was at their first meeting, after being re-opened, that they received a copy in *manuscript* of the address and resolulutions of the London Corresponding Society. The envelope was signed by Hardy, but the address itself had no signature; and as the Constitutional Society resolved to publish it, it is probable that Mr. Tooke put Hardy's name to it before it was entered in the books, and sent to the newspapers. That circumstance is sufficient to account for the mystery which so puzzled the Attorney General, why the name of *Thomas Hardy, Secretary,* was in the hand writing of *Mr. Tooke.* The address thus signed was seized among the papers of Mr. Adams, Secretary to the Constitutional Society; and from that circumstance and others, equally mistaken, jumbled together, the Attorney General inferred and asserted, that the London Corresponding Society was modelled by the Constitutional Society—meaning Tooke, and Felix Vaughan. Gurney's Report has the same in substance, at pages 69, 77, and 78.

At this period he had some leisure from his usual employment, and he occupied the time in re-perusing a collection of political tracts, published by the Society for Constitutional Information, in the years 1779, 1780, 1781, 1782, and 1783, which had been presented to him by a Member of that Society, T. B. Hollis, Esq. This drew his attention more closely to the subjects on which he had been accustomed to think and talk a great deal during the American war. He drew up some rules, with a preamble to them, for the management of the Society which he had projected. These rules he submitted to three friends, whom he engaged to supper with him one night, with a view of obtaining their opinions on the subject. His friends highly approved of them, as proper fundamental regulations for a Society, whose efforts were to be employed in endeavouring to restore to Britons those civil rights of which they had been deprived by the unholy union of force and fraud, at various periods, and by all parties that had obtained power—Whigs, then, as well as Tories.

These outlines being agreed upon between him and his three friends, they, next, resolved to meet weekly in future at a public house, and to invite as many of their friends as they thought were likely to exert themselves in promoting the object of the Society.

"What great events arise from little things!"

This Society, consisting at first of no more than four members, plain homely citizens, soon acquired an influence, and encreased to a magnitude too well known to require any particular description.

However, it is necessary to follow its progress a little. In the beginning of January, 1792, the first meeting was held at the sign of the Bell, in Exeter Street, in the Strand, when there were present only nine persons, all acquainted with each other. They had finished their daily labour, and met there by appointment. After having had their bread and cheese and porter for supper, as usual, and their pipes afterwards, with some conversation on the hardness of the times and the dearness of all the necessaries of life, which they, in common with their fellow citizens, felt to their sorrow, the business for which they had met was brought forward—*Parliamentary Reform*—an important subject to be deliberated upon, and dealt with by such a class of men. Hardy then produced the rules and preamble which he had drawn out; and after they had been read twice, it was proposed that all who wished to become members should subscribe them, and engage to endeavour, by all the means in their power, to promote the objects the Society had in view. To this proposal all present, except one man, readily agreed. This man said he would take a week to consider of it; and he also became a member at the next meeting. Hardy presented a book which he had bought for the purpose, that those who became members might put down their names, and pay one penny, which was to be continued weekly, as one of the rules expresses.

There was some conversation about what name should be given to the Society; some would have it called "The Patriotic Club," some the "Reformation Society," when Hardy shewed them some cards upon which he had written "The London Corresponding Society, No. 1, 2, 3, &c.;" and that denomination was unanimously adopted. Hardy was then appointed Secretary and Treasurer. There were eight persons who had subscribed the rules, and paid a penny each, consequently there was eight pence in the treasury,—a mighty sum! Next weekly meeting, nine more joined the Society, which encreased the fund to two shillings and one penny. The third meeting brought an accession of twenty-four new members, which made the treasury rich to the important amount of four shillings and one penny.

The first correspondence of the Society was the following letter, addressed by Hardy to the Rev. Mr. Bryant, of Sheffield. It was private; but, on reading that gentleman's answer to the assembled members, the transaction was adopted as that of the whole body. The letter is here inserted, because, on the trial, the Attorney General, now Lord Eldon, lamented very much —he is good at lamentations—that he had not possession of it, and because the reply which it elicited tended very much to animate the Corresponding Society in the great cause of *Parliamentary* Reform.

London, 8th March, 1792.

REVEREND SIR,

I hope you will pardon that freedom which I take in troubling you with the following sentiments; nothing but the importance of the business could have induced me to address one who is an entire stranger to me, except *only* by report. Hearing from my friend, Gustavus Vassa, the African, who is now writing memoirs of his life in my house, that you are a zealous friend to the abolition of that cursed traffic, the Slave Trade, I infer, from that circumstance, *that you are a zealous friend to freedom on the broad basis of the* RIGHTS OF MAN. I am fully persuaded that there is no man, who is, from principle, an advocate for the liberty of the black man, but will zealously support the rights of the white man, and *vice versa.*

The reason why I write to you, at this time, is this. There are some tradesmen, mechanics, and shopkeepers here in London, forming a Society for a Reform in Parliament, which, in our opinion, is of all other things most deserving the attention of the public. We are more and more convinced, from every day's experience, that the restoring the right of voting to every man, not incapacitated by nature for want of reason, nor by law for the commission of crimes, together with annual election, is the only reform that can be effectual and permanent. It has been a long, and very just complaint, that a very great majority of the people of this country are not represented in Parliament; that the majority of the House of Commons are chosen by a number of voters, not exceeding twelve thousand; and that many large and populous towns have not a single vote for a representative: such as Birmingham, containing upwards of 40,000 inhabitants; Manchester, above 30,000; Leeds, above 20,000; besides Sheffield, Bradford, Halifax, Wolverhampton, &c. &c. &c.; since that estimate of the inhabitants was made, their number has been more than doubled. The views and intentions of this Society are directed towards ascertaining the opinion, and to know the determination, as far as possible, of the unrepresented part of the people. From these considerations we have taken the name of

The London Corresponding Society, for restoring the right of suffrage to the unrepresented of the people of Great Britain. The following are our leading rules. That the number of our Members be unlimited. That no one can become a Member unless he be proposed by one of the Members and seconded by another. That he be above the age of twenty years, and resident in Great Britain one year. And to be esteemed a Member of the Society, it is requisite that he pay, at least, *one penny* a week, towards defraying the necessary expenses of the Society. I have here given you some of our reasons and motives for associating, and our terms of admission. Since we did associate, we have heard that there are Societies also forming in Sheffield for promoting the same important cause.

As I do not know either the President, or the Secretary, and presuming you are a Member, I trust you will oblige me with all the information you judge prudent, concerning the government of your Society, as ours is not yet perfectly organized. Any information from you, or the Society at Sheffield, tending to facilitate the grand and ultimate end, or even any advice, will be gratefully received by him who begs leave to subscribe himself,

Reverend Sir,
Your most obedient and most
Humble Servant,
THOMAS HARDY.

4, *Taylor's Buildings,*
   St. Martin's Lane.

On the 2nd of April, 1792, the London Corresponding Society came before the public with an address and resolutions, in which their principles and views were clearly and unequivocally stated. This first address was written by Mr. Margarot; and it was judged requisite and proper that some person should sign it as Chairman; more especially as it was their first public act. It was proposed to several persons to allow their names to appear, but some objected, and others pleaded private reasons, best known to themselves, in excuse. However, as the Society deemed it necessary to have a name, it was at last proposed to Hardy to allow his to appear. He had no other objection than the probability that it might prove prejudicial to the Society, to have their first document published under the sanction of so obscure a name. This objection was overruled, and his name alone, as Secretary, appeared to the first Address and Resolutions, of which the following is a true copy :—

LONDON CORRESPONDING SOCIETY,

Held at the Bell, Exeter Street, Strand.

MAN, as an individual, is entitled to liberty—it is his birthright.

As a member of society, the preservation of that liberty becomes his indispensable duty.

When he associated, he gave up certain rights, in order to secure the possession of the remainder;

But, he voluntarily yielded up only as much as was necessary for the common good:

He still preserved a right of sharing in the government of his country;—without it, no man can with truth call himself FREE.

Fraud or force, sanctioned by custom, with-holds that right from (by far) the greater number of the inhabitants of this country.

The few with whom the right of election and representation remains, abuse it, and the strong temptations held out to electors, sufficiently prove that the representatives of this country seldom procure a seat in Parliament, from the *unbought* suffrages of a free people.

The nation at length perceives it, and testifies an ardent desire of remedying the evil.

The only difficulty, therefore, at present is, the ascertaining the true method of proceeding.

To this end, different and numerous Societies have been formed in various parts of the nation.

Several likewise have arisen in the Metropolis; and among them, (though as yet in its infant state) the LONDON CORRESPONDING SOCIETY, with modesty intrudes itself and opinions, on the attention of the public, in the following Resolutions;

1. *Resolved*,—That every individual has a right to share in the government of that Society of which he is a Member—unless incapacitated:

2. *Resolved*,—That nothing but non-age, privation of reason, or an offence against the general rules of society, can incapacitate him.

3. *Resolved*,—That it is no less the RIGHT than the DUTY of every citizen, to keep a watchful eye on the government of his country; that the laws, by being multiplied, do not degenerate into *Oppression*; and that those who are entrusted with the Government, do not substitute *Private Interest* for *Public Advantage*.

4. *Resolved*,—That the people of Great Britain are not *effectually* represented in Parliament.

5. *Resolved*,—That in consequence of a *partial, unequal,* and therefore *inadequate Representation*, together with the *corrupt* method in which Representatives are elected; *oppressive taxes, unjust laws, restrictions of liberty,* and *wasting of the public money,* have ensued.

6. *Resolved*,—That the only remedy to those evils is a fair, equal, and impartial Representation of the people in Parliament.

7. *Resolved*,—That a fair, equal, and impartial Representation can never take place, until all *partial privileges* are abolished.

8. *Resolved*,—That this Society do express their *abhorrence* of tumult and violence; and that, as they aim at Reform, not anarchy; reason, firmness, and unanimity are the only arms they themselves will employ, or persuade their fellow-citizens to exert, against ABUSE OF POWER.

Ordered,—That the Secretary of this Society do transmit a copy of the above to the Societies for Constitutional Information, established in *London, Sheffield*, and *Manchester*.

By Order of the Committee,

T. HARDY, Secretary.

April 2, 1792.

A copy of these Resolutions was sent to the Society for Constitutional Information, as already mentioned, and they were, by that Society, published in the newspapers. They were afterwards published by the London Corresponding Society itself, in the form of hand-bills, and thousands of them distributed in London, and throughout the country.

It was about this period that Hardy became acquainted with a gentleman, whose acquaintance and friendship was a real honour—J. Horne Tooke—that steady and intrepid champion of freedom; that unflinching supporter of Parliamentary Reform; and with many others of the friends of that cause, which promised peace and happiness to their fellow men. These virtuous men have been since falsely represented by successive governments and their hirelings, as traitors and enemies to their country; a dark and shameful blot on the annals of this civilized land, that its destinies should be confided to the management of men, either so ignorant or so wicked! The discerning and unprejudiced part of the nation, however, see clearly who are, and who have been the real enemies of their country; who have been aiding and abetting the robbery and murder of their fellow creatures, both at home and abroad. And these are the men who have been active in slandering and persecuting the friends of justice and humanity. He acquired the acquaintance of Thomas Paine, also, about the same time; a man whose political writings, especially his celebrated "Rights of Man," seemed to electrify the nation, and terrified the imbecile government of the day into the most desperate and unjustifiable measures.

The next transaction of the London Corresponding Society, was a congratulatory Address to the National Convention of France, of which the following is a copy. It was confided to the French Ambassador, who was, soon after, suddenly ordered to quit this country. In the Convention it was received with rapturous applause, as the first address from this country; and was afterwards one of the documents brought against the prisoners tried for High Treason. The National Convention distributed printed copies throughout all the Departments of France, where it caused a very great sensation.

The London Corresponding Society's Congratulatory Address to the National Convention of France.

" Frenchmen,

" WHILE foreign robbers are ravaging your territories, under the specious pretext of justice, cruelty and desolation leading on their van, perfidy, with treachery, bringing up their rear; yet mercy and friendship, impudently held forth to the world as the sole motives of their incursions, the oppressed part of mankind forgetting, for a while, their own sufferings, feel only for yours, and with an anxious eye watch the event, fervently supplicating the Almighty Ruler of the universe to be favourable to your cause, so intimately blended with their own.

" Frowned upon by an oppressive system of controul, whose gradual, but continued encroachments, have deprived this nation of nearly all its boasted liberty, and brought us almost to that abject state of slavery, from which you have so emerged, 5,000 British citizens, indignant, manfully step forth to rescue their country from the opprobrium brought upon it by the supine conduct of those in power. They conceive it to be the duty of Britons to countenance and assist to the utmost of their power, the champions of human happiness, and to swear to a nation, proceeding on the plan you have adopted, an inviolable friendship. Sacred from this day be that friendship between us! and may vengeance to the uttermost, overtake the man who hereafter shall attempt to cause a rupture.

" Though we appear so few at present, be assured, Frenchmen, that our number encreases daily; it is true, that the stern uplifted arm of authority at present keeps back the timid, that busily circulated impostors hourly mislead the credulous, and that Court intimacy, with avowed French traitors, has some effect on the unwary, and on the ambitious. But, with certainty, we can inform you, friends and freemen, that information makes a rapid progress among us. Curiosity has taken possession of the public mind; the conjoint reign of ignorance and despotism passes away. Men now ask each other, What is freedom? What are our rights? Frenchmen, you are already free, and Britons are preparing to become so.

" Casting far from us the criminal prejudices artfully inculcated by evil-minded men, and wily Courtiers, we, instead of natural enemies, at length discover in Frenchmen our fellow citizens of the world, and our brethren by the same Heavenly Father, who created us for the purpose of loving and mutually assisting each other; but not to hate, and to be ever ready to cut each others throats, at the commands of weak or ambitious Kings, and corrupt Ministers.

" Seeking our real enemies, we find them in our bosoms, we feel ourselves inwardly torn by, and ever the victims of a restless, all consuming aristocracy, hitherto the bane of every nation under the sun! Wisely have you acted in expelling it from France.

"Warm as our wishes for your success, eager as we are to behold freedom triumphant, and man every where restored to the enjoyment of his just rights, a sense of our duty, as orderly citizens, forbids our flying in arms to your assistance; our government has pledged the national faith to remain neutral:—in a struggle of liberty against Despotism, Britons remain neutral! oh shame! But we have entrusted our King with discretionary powers!—we, therefore, must obey;—our hands are bound, but our hearts are free, and they are with you.

"Let German despots act as they please. We shall rejoice at their fall, compassionating however their enslaved subjects. We hope this tyranny of their masters will prove the means of reinstating, in the full enjoyment of their rights and liberties, millions of our fellow creatures.

"With unconcern, therefore, we view the Elector of Hanover join his troops to traitors and robbers; but the King of Great Britain will do well to remember, that this country is not Hanover.—Should he forget this distinction, we will not.

"While you enjoy the envied glory of being the unaided defenders of freedom, we fondly anticipate, in idea, the numerous blessings mankind will enjoy; if you succeed, as we ardently wish, the triple alliance (not of Crowns, but) of the people of America, France, and Britain, will give freedom to Europe, and peace to the whole world. Dear friends, you combat for the advantage of the human race. How well purchased will be, though at the expense of much blood, the glorious, the unprecedented privilege of saying mankind is free! Tyrants and tyranny are no more! Peace reigns on the earth! And this is the work of Frenchmen!

"The desire of having the concurrence of different Societies to this Address, has occasioned a month's delay in presenting it. Success, unparallelled, has now attended your arms. We congratulate you thereon. That success has removed our anxiety, but it has no otherwise influenced our sentiments in your behalf. Remember, Frenchmen, that although this testimony of friendship only now reaches your Assembly, it bears date the 27th September, 1792."

(Signed by Order)

   MAURICE MARGAROT, President.
   THOMAS HARDY, Secretary.

We now arrive at a period which draws the subject of this Memoir forth from the humble occupation of a shoemaker, in which he had hitherto laboured with great credit to himself, to take his stand by the side of those immortal heroes, in whose praise the tongues of Britons will never cease to speak with rapture and grateful veneration. With that patriotic band who broke the ruffian arm of arbitrary power, and dyed the field and the scaffold with their pure and precious blood, for the liberties of their country,—Hampden, Russell, Sidney; ye intrepid martyrs to freedom! All hail to your ever glorious memory! Alas! how near was the page of our history to being again stained with the record of another bloody tragedy, similar to that which terminated your bright and honourable career! But, thanks to the firmness and integrity of twelve honest Britons, the page which was again intended for so foul a record has been preserved pure, and, for the happiness of millions, has been made the splendid recorder of the triumph of truth and justice.

But to return to the subject, from which the warmth of honest feeling has caused us to digress. Before the end of the year 1792, such is the prevalence of truth, and such is the weight and force of her arguments, the London Corresponding Society, to which Hardy was still Secretary, formed an intimate connexion, and had frequent correspondence with every Society in Great Britain, which had been instituted for the purpose of obtaining, by legal and constitutional means, a Reform in the Commons' House of Parliament. The correspondence with these Societies, and with others which continued to be daily forming, in all parts of England and Scotland, was regular, until they were deranged in November, by the starting up of a Society, hostile to liberty, under the denomination of " An Association for protecting property against republicans and levellers," which met at the Crown and Anchor Tavern. This Society was not merely countenanced, but actually appointed by the Ministers of that day, for the express purpose of calumniating the best friends of the country, that they might plunder and tyrannize, uncontrolled, over the people, in which, in a great measure, they succeeded. John Reeves, Charles Yorke, and Mr. Devaynes, were at the head of the Association.

In this deranged state of the London Corresponding Society, they published an Address to the Nation, vindicating their character from the base lies propagated against them by the new Association, every member of which was interested in preventing Reform. The whole body, with their connexions, were, in fact, plundering the nation of millions, which has since been clearly proved; so that if a Reform had taken place at that time, these few worthless individuals would have been reduced to comparative poverty, and the nation saved. Mr. Margarot signed the Address as Chairman, and Hardy as Secretary. The copies were printed in the form of large broadsides, and posted up in various parts of London. As a preliminary to what was to be expected to follow, the bill-sticker was apprehended, and afterwards tried, found guilty, and sentenced to six months imprisonment and a fine, which was paid by the Society. The Address is here given at length, that the present generation may see the severity with which liberal principles were dealt with in the days of their fathers, and that if these fathers did not recover the liberty that had been wrested from their ancestors, it was not for want of struggling, and braving every danger in the cause. It was written by Felix Vaughan, Esq. Barrister at Law, and Member of the Society.

ADDRESS

OF THE

LONDON CORRESPONDING SOCIETY,

To the other Societies of Great Britain,

UNITED FOR THE OBTAINING A

REFORM IN PARLIAMENT.

FRIENDS, AND FELLOW COUNTRYMEN,

UNLESS we are greatly deceived, the time is approaching when the object for which we struggle is likely to come within our reach.—That a nation like Britain should be free, it is requisite only that Britons should will it to become so; that such should be their will, the abuses of our *original Constitution*, and the alarm of our aristocratic enemies, sufficiently witness.—Confident in the purity of our motives, and in the justice of our cause, let us meet falsehood with proofs, and hypocrisy with plainness.—Let us persevere in declaring our principles, and Misrepresentation will meet its due reward—Contempt.

In this view the artifices of a late ARISTOCRATIC ASSOCIATION, formed on the 20th instant, call for a few remarks, on account of the declaration they have published relative to other Clubs and Societies formed in this nation; it is true that this meeting of *gentlemen* (for so they style themselves), have mentioned no names, instanced no facts, quoted no authorities; but they take upon themselves to assert, that bodies of their countrymen have been associated, professing opinions favourable to the RIGHTS OF MAN, TO LIBERTY AND EQUALITY; and moreover that those opinions are conveyed in the terms NO KING! NO PARLIAMENT! —So much for their assertions.

If this be intended to include the Societies to which we respectively belong, we here, in the most solemn manner, deny the latter part of the charge; while, in admitting the former, we claim the privilege, and glory in the character of Britons. Whoever shall attribute to us (who wish only the restoration of the lost liberties of our country) the expressions of NO KING! NO PARLIAMENT! or any design of invading the PROPERTY of other men, is guilty of a wilful, an impudent, and a malicious falsehood.

We know and are sensible that the wages of every man are his right; that *difference of strength, of talents, and of industry, do and ought to afford proportional distinctions of property, which,* when acquired and confirmed by the laws, *is sacred and inviolable.* We defy the most slavish and malevolent man in the meeting of the 20th instant, to bring the remotest proof to the contrary. If there be no proof, we call upon them to justify an insidious calumny, which seems invented only to terrify independent Britons from reclaiming the *rightful Constitution of their country.*

We admit and we declare, that we are friends to CIVIL LIBERTY, and therefore to NATURAL EQUALITY, both of which we consider as the RIGHTS OF MANKIND —could we believe them to be *" in direct opposition to the laws of this land,"* we should blush to find ourselves among the number of its inhabitants; but we are persuaded that the abuses of the constitution will never pass current for its true principles, since we are told in its first Charter that all are EQUAL in the *sight of the law,* which *" shall neither be sold, nor refused, nor delayed, to any free man whatsoever."* Should it ever happen that " RIGHT AND JUSTICE" are opposed by expence, by refusal, or by delay, THEN IS THIS PRINCIPLE OF EQUALITY VIOLATED, AND WE ARE NO LONGER FREEMEN.

Such are our notions of those rights, which it is boldly maintained are "*inconsistent with the well-being of Society.*" But let us not suffer men who avow no principles of liberty, whose favourite cry is INEQUALITY OF PROPERTY, to estrange others of our countrymen from aiding us in serving the community, and from recovering to the nation that share of its sovereignty, which has unhappily been sacrificed to CORRUPT COURTIERS and intriguing BOROUGH MONGERS.

If our laws and constitution be just and wise in their origin and their principle, every deviation from them as first established must be injurious to the people, whose persons and property were then secured; if, at the Revolution, this country was adequately represented, it is now so no longer, and therefore calls aloud for REFORM.

If it be true that the people of Britain are superior to other nations, is it that our taxes are less burthensome, or that our provisions are less expensive? Is it from the various productions of our soil that we are rich? Is it owing to the majority of our numbers that we are strong? Certainly not! France has the advantage in all these respects, and up to this period she has never been our superior in wealth, in power, in talents, or in virtues. But let us not deceive ourselves; the difference between us and that nation was, formerly, that our Monarchy was limited, while theirs was absolute; that the number of our aristocracy did not equal the thousandth part of theirs; that we had Trial by Jury, while they had none; that our persons were protected by the laws, while their lives were at the mercy of every titled individual. We, therefore, had that to fight for, which to them was unknown, since we were MEN while they were SLAVES.

The scene indeed has changed: like our brave ancestors of the last century, they have driven out the family that would have destroyed them; they have scattered the mercenaries who invaded their freedom, " and have broken their chains on the heads of their oppressors." If during this conflict with military assassins and domestic traitors, cruelty and revenge have arisen among a few inhabitants of the capital, let us lament these effects of a bloody and tyrannous MANIFESTO; but let us leave to the hypocrite pretenders to humanity, the task of blackening the misfortune, and attributing to a whole nation the act of an enraged populace.

As we have never yet been cast so low at the foot of despotism, so is it not requisite that we should appeal to the same awful tribunal with our brethren on the Continent. May our enmities be written in sand, but may our rights be engraven on marble! We desire to overthrow no property but what has been raised on the RUINS OF OUR LIBERTY! We look with reverence on the landed and commercial interests of our country; but we view with abhorrence that MONOPOLY of BURGAGE TENURES, unwarranted by law or reason, in this or any other nation in Europe.

Let us then continue, with patience and firmness, in the path which is begun; let us then wait and watch the ensuing Sessions of Parliament, from whom we have much to hope, and little to fear. The House of Commons may have been the source of our calamity; it may prove that of our deliverance. Should it not, we trust we shall not prove unworthy of our forefathers, WHOSE EXERTIONS IN THE CAUSE OF MANKIND SO WELL DESERVE OUR IMITATION.

M. MARGAROT, *Chairman.*
T. HARDY, *Secretary.*

The signing of this Address, though it was so public, and its principles, it is to be hoped, were those of every rational being, was brought against Hardy as an act of High Treason. Other documents, equally devoid of treason, were also brought against him, some of which shall be hereafter noticed; but to notice them all would be to republish the Attorney General's speech, which took him nine hours to deliver.

In the Spring of the year 1793, petitions were promoted by the different Constitutional Societies in their respective towns and neighbourhoods, not in their capacities of members of the Societies, but as members of the community deprived of their rights, and desiring that those rights might be restored to them.

These petitions were presented to the House of Commons, for the purpose of strengthening Mr. Grey's motion for Reform. Some of them were read and animadverted upon with great asperity by many of the members of that House, for speaking with a bolder tone of remonstrance than was agreeable to the prejudices and opinions of a great majority of them. These, of course, were all rejected. Others, less offensive, were ordered to lie on the table, or, in other words, were consigned to oblivion without observation.

In October, 1793, a Convention of the different Societies of Scotland was held in Edinburgh, with the view of obtaining the Reformation of Parliament; previously to which Mr. Skirving, the Secretary, wrote to Mr. Hardy, Secretary to the London Corresponding Society, requesting that Society to send delegates to the Convention in Scotland, and also a request that he and the other members would use their influence with other English Societies to do the like. A similar letter was sent, by Mr. Skirving, to the London and Sheffield Constitutional Societies, with a similar request, all of which requests were complied with; and these three Societies, on the 9th of November, 1793, sent delegates accordingly.

It is almost unnecessary to say any thing upon a subject so well known; but as the thread of our story requires to be preserved unbroken, we shall be as concise as possible. The Convention met in Edinburgh on the 19th of November, 1793; the delegates of the three English Societies being of the number that attended. They proceeded to business with a regularity, decorum, and dignity, by no means unworthy of the imitation of *assemblies* of a much longer standing. They met with no interruption for upwards of a fortnight. Their proceedings were open to the public at large, and their resolutions debated and adopted in the presence of all who chose to attend. A short time after the meeting of the Convention, Mr. Margarot, delegate from the London Corresponding Society, received authority from the United Societies of Norwich to act for them; and Mr. C. Brown, from the Sheffield Society, received a similar commission from the Society at Leeds. Every week fresh Societies were springing up, even to the utmost parts of Scotland, and sending delegates to Edinburgh to the Convention. The eyes of the whole nation were so anxiously and steadily fixed upon its proceedings, that the servants of Government became alarmed, and all at once, in defiance of justice, the law of Scotland, and in the face of Magna Charta, and the Bill of Rights, the Magistrates of Edinburgh, attended by a posse of constables, thief catchers, and others, armed with bludgeons, pistols, and hangers, invaded the Convention, and insisted on dispersing it, which, after some struggle, they effected. What followed, is well known. The English delegates were all held to bail, and some of them indicted. Margarot and Gerald were tried for sedition; and with Skirving, the Secretary to the Scottish Societies and Convention, Thomas Muir, and F. Palmer, were convicted, and sentenced to fourteen years transportation to Botany Bay.

The English Societies, whose rights had been thus wantonly trampled upon, in the severe and unjust punishment inflicted upon their delegates, held frequent meetings, and passed some strong resolutions on the subject, expressive of their indignation; and after many consultations and communications, it was at length resolved to call another Convention to be held in England, and to which the Scottish Societies should be requested to send delegates. The English Ministers being advised, through their *spies* and *informers*, that this measure was about to be adopted, took the alarm, and employed such means to prevent it as reflect disgrace upon their memories, and astonished, not only Great Britain, but also all Europe.

On the memorable 12th of May, 1794, at half-past six o'clock in the morning, Mr. Lazun, junior, the son of the King's messenger of that name, and who was himself afterwards made an assistant messenger, as a reward for his activity on that occasion, gave a thundering knock at the door, No. 9, Piccadilly, before the shop was opened; and Hardy, having no suspicion of what had been prepared for him, jumped out of bed, and went, half-dressed, to see what could be the matter at that early hour. Upon the door being opened, Lazun rushed in, followed by John Gurnel, the King's messenger, P. Macmanus, and John Townsend, Bow Street officers—better known by the appellation of thief takers—Mr. John King, private Secretary to Mr. Dundas, and two or three others whose names Hardy did not learn. Lazun seized him, and proceeded to search his pockets, where he found some letters and papers, besides his pocket book, containing two bills of exchange to the amount of £196. Hardy desired to know by what authority he was thus treated, when Lazun shewed him a paper, which he called a warrant for his apprehension, on a charge of High Treason: but before he could read more than a few lines, the young upstart in authority, re-folded, and put it again in his pocket. He observed, however, something about High Treason, connected with his own name, but had not an opportunity then of observing by whom it was signed.

Lazun was very active in rumaging all the drawers, even those containing Mrs. Hardy's clothes. He demanded the key of a bureau, which happened to be locked, and when he found he could not obtain it, he threatened to break it, and proceeded to put his threat in execution by trying to force it open with the poker. Mrs. Hardy entreated him to desist, and Mr. King called in a smith, who was in waiting, with a box full of all sorts of picklocks, and skeleton keys. This man did his business very expeditiously. He picked the lock of the bureau, and those of some trunks, and the party soon had four large silk handkerchiefs filled with letters and other papers; among which were many of Hardy's private letters from friends in America, and at home. Mr. King then called a hackney coach, which was in attendance, into which Mr. Hardy and the four bundles of papers were put, accompanied by Gurnel and Townsend, and carried to the messenger's house in King Street, corner of Charles Street, Westminster. The rest of the party remained behind, at No. 9, Piccadilly, and, not content with manuscripts, took as many books and pamphlets as nearly filled a *corn sack,* without *marking* one article.

The feelings of poor Mrs. Hardy, on that occasion, may be easier imagined than described. In an advanced state of pregnancy, sitting in bed all the time, and unable to dress before so many unwelcome visitors, whom she could hardly consider in a better light than that of robbers.

Hardy remained in the custody of Mr. Gurnel, by whom, and his family, he was civilly treated, from the 12th to the 29th of May. During that time he underwent several examinations before the Privy Council, consisting of Messrs. Pitt, and Dundas, the Duke of Montrose, the Marquis of Stafford, Lords Grenville, Hawkesbury, and Salisbury, the Lord Chancellor, the Attorney and Solicitor General, White, Solicitor to the Treasury, John Reeves, of notorious memory, Falkner, &c.

The first examination took place at eleven o'clock on the morning on which he was taken; when, being asked by Mr. Dundas his name and occupation, he gave a ready answer. He was then asked many questions to which he could not reply; and many letters and papers were shewn to him which he had never seen before, and of which, of course, he knew nothing; but the letters and papers he had written and signed, he readily acknowledged. On Tuesday and Wednesday his examination was continued; but he was not again called before the Council until Monday, when he was questioned about guns, pikes, and other warlike instruments. Of such instruments he knew nothing. It is impossible that so many Societies as then existed, could be without some violent characters, among which might be included the Government spies; but whatever such unworthy persons may have hinted, in any of the numerous Societies, about arms, Hardy, and the real patriotic part of them, abhorred the very idea of having recourse to violence of any sort. All their efforts were directed to the recovery of the lost rights of themselves and of their fellow citizens—in fact, to the attainment of Parliamentary Reform, by constitutional and peaceable means.

On the very day of Hardy's capture, a Message from the King was brought down to the Commons, by Mr. Dundas, announcing that the seditious practices which had been for some time carried on by certain Societies in London, in correspondence with Societies in different parts of the country, had lately been pursued with increased activity and boldness, and had been avowedly directed to the object of assembling a general convention of the people, in contempt and defiance of the authority of Parliament, and on principles subversive of the existing laws and Constitution, and directly tending to the introduction of that system of anarchy and confusion which had *fatally prevailed in France*. That, in consequence, his Majesty had given directions for seizing the books and papers of the said Societies in London, which had been seized accordingly; and that these books and papers, appearing to contain matters of great importance to the public, his Majesty had given orders for laying them before the House of Commons; and his Majesty recommended it to the House to consider the same, and to take such measures thereupon as might appear to be necessary, for effectually guarding against the further prosecution of those dangerous designs, and for preserving to his Majesty's subjects the *enjoyment of the blessings* derived to them by the Constitution happily established in these kingdoms.

On the 14th, a Committee was appointed for examining the papers, which Committee was afterwards accused, and not without apparent reason, of falsifying and garbling the documents. On the 16th, Mr. Pitt brought up the Report, and moved " for leave to bring in a bill to empower his Majesty to secure and detain all such persons as shall be suspected of conspiring against his person and Government:" which, after an animated debate, during which the House divided thirteen times, was granted. After another debate, in which the minority, though small, displayed splendid talents, the bills passed, of course. On the 17th, a similar Message was presented by Lord Grenville, from his Majesty, to the House of Lords, when the Ministers were attacked by the Duke of Grafton, and Lord Stanhope. The latter nobleman defended the Societies. " These papers," said he, " are written by a set of men, honest in their intentions, though not rich, nor of high rank. They may, from a defect of education, have been somewhat inaccurate in their expressions—(the Ministers laughed at this); but their intentions were clearly legal, as their professed aim was to obtain a redress of grievances by legal means.

The bill for suspending the Habeas Corpus passed the Lords on the 22d of May, and was protested against by the following noblemen:—Earl Stanhope, Duke of Bedford, the Earls of Albemarle, Lauderdale, and Derby.

In spite, however, of all these severe measures, it is pretty clear, had this country remained at peace, that nothing short of an extensive and efficient Reform would have satisfied the people. The Ministers were " wise in their generation ;" they saw this, and, with a view of diverting the public mind from the subject, plunged the country into a destructive war, which has caused an accumulation of debt and misery, dreadful to contemplate. The industrious have complained, and have had oppression added to oppression. They have been answered as Rehoboam answered the people of Israel:—" My Father hath chastised you with whips, but I will chastise you with scorpions." And what was the consequence? The people said, " what portion have we in David? neither have we inheritance in the son of Jesse. To your tents, O Israel; now see to thine own house David. So Israel rebelled against the House of David unto this day."—1 Kings, chapter xii. verses 16, 19.

But to resume our subject. Hardy was, on the 29th of May, 1794, committed to the Tower, on a warrant from the Privy Council, on a charge of High Treason, with orders that none should be admitted to see him, except such as brought a precept for that purpose, from those under whose authority he was committed. After some days had elapsed, the faithful partner of his bosom, who has been already mentioned as far advanced in a state of pregnancy, obtained permission, by virtue of such precept, to pay him a mournful visit, and was allowed after to see him twice a week; but not to remain with him more than two hours at a time; sometimes no more than one, and that always in the presence of the Gaoler, one of the Wardens, or a Serjeant, whom the Gaoler ordered to prevent any private conversation inaudible to him. If they happened to whisper, they were told to speak up, that they might be heard.

In the mean time, the newspapers, particularly the TIMES NEWSPAPER, teemed with the most wicked and shameful misrepresentation of the views and intentions of the unfortunate prisoner. He was loaded with every degree of calumnious accusations, with a view of inflaming and prejudicing the public mind against him. Even his innocent and unprotected family was persecuted with the most dastardly and unmanly rancour. The following well known fact will evince this beyond contradiction. It happened on the 11th of June, 1794, the night on which the illumination took place in London, to commemorate Lord Howe's victory over the French fleet. On that night a large mob of ruffians assembled before his house, No. 9, Piccadilly, and without any ceremony began to assail the windows with stones and brick-bats. These were very soon demolished, although there had been lights up as in the adjoining houses. They next attempted to break open the shop door, and swore, with the most horrid oaths, that they would either burn or pull down the house. The unfortunate Mrs. Hardy was within, with no other protector than an old woman who attended her as nurse. Weak and enfeebled as she was, from her personal situation, and from what she must have suffered on account of her husband, it is no wonder that she should have been terrified by the threats and assaults of such a crowd of infuriated desperadoes. We have seen the readiness with which the military have been sent to the aid of the civil power, to preserve crimping houses, but neither civil nor military power interfered to preserve the property of this persecuted man, nor that of the exalted patriot, Lord Stanhope, from the violence of a lawless mob, more than suspected of having been hired for the base purpose.

Mrs. Hardy called to the neighbours who lived at the back of the house, and who were in a state of great anxiety for her safety, in case the villains should have effected their purpose of breaking into the premises. They advised her to make her way through a small back window, on the ground floor, which she accordingly attempted, but being very large round the waist, she stuck fast in it, and it was only by main force that she could be dragged through, much injured by the bruises which she received: and as, when brought to bed, soon afterwards, the child was dead, it may reasonably be concluded that it lost its life by the violent compression which the unfortunate mother suffered in that afflicting business.

The unceasing and merciless system of defamation which continued to be pursued against her husband, had such an evident effect upon the mind of Mrs Hardy, that her health began rapidly to decline; yet she strove to appear as cheerful as possible, and continued her visits to the Tower, as often as she was permitted, until the very day of her death. On the 27th of August, 1794, she was taken in labour, and delivered of a dead child. She declared, soon afterwards, that she found her own death fast approaching, and that she believed it to be entirely owing to what she had suffered in her person, and in her mind, on account of the confinement of her husband. About two o'clock of the same day she had parted with her husband, in as good spirits as was possible in her situation—took her last farewell—it was her last—for they were doomed never to see each other again in this vale of tears.

The following is the beginning of a letter which Mrs. Hardy was writing to her husband, a few hours before she died, August 27th, 1794; but a summons of eternal importance to her own soul obliged her to drop the pen without finishing it.

"My dear Hardy,

"This comes with my tenderest affection for you. You are never out of my thoughts, sleeping or waking. Oh, to think what companions you have with you! None that you can converse with either on temporal or spiritual matters; but I hope the Spirit of God is both with you and me, and I pray that he may give us grace to look up to Christ. There all the good is that we can either hope or wish for, if we have but faith and patience, although we are but poor sinful mortals. My dear, you have it not in——"

To describe the state of the unfortunate prisoner's feelings, on receiving the mournful account of his loss, next morning, would be impossible. Let us think better of human nature than to suppose it necessary. The reader who can peruse the tragic story without a double emotion of indignation and pity, is not to be envied his feelings.

The following beautiful poem, written by " A friend to the distressed Patriots," appeared some time afterwards, and merits a place here. The author, Citizen Lee, went to America, in 1796, and died soon after. He wrote many beautiful poems, which have been published in several volumes. Free for ever be the land which afforded an asylum and a grave to the patriot bard!

ON THE DEATH OF MRS. HARDY,

Wife of Mr. Thomas Hardy, of Piccadilly;

IMPRISONED IN THE TOWER ON A CHARGE OF HIGH TREASON.

She expired in Child-bed, on Wednesday, August 27, 1794; and declared, in her last moments, that she died a martyr to the sufferings of her husband.

Exalted hero! glory of my verse;
THY WEIGHTY SUFFERINGS! would the Muse rehearse!
With melting lays obtain the listening ear,
And draw from Pity's eye the pearly tear.
I see thee, fetter'd in tyrannic chains,
Thy spirit laden with a thousand pains;
Yet heedless to the mighty load of woe,
No plaint is heard, no tears are seen to flow;
The pleasing hope of bringing SLAVES RELIEF,
Inspires thy gen'rous soul, and lulls thy grief.
On Heav'n reclining, still thou hop'st to see
All tyrants dead, and heav'n-born LIBERTY
Her gentle sway extending all around,
Each human forehead with her LAURELS crown'd!
   But why art thou enchain'd? What hellish might
Presum'd to rob thee of thy dearest right?
To rob the world? So good a man confin'd,
He suffers not alone, but all mankind!
'Twas TYRANNY'S FELL DEED; his haggard eyes,
Saw truth in thee, reflected from the skies;
Bright as the morning planet, with her light,
Chasing the shadows of retreating night;
And trembled lest the SECRETS should be known,
That are in HELL conceal'd and prop his Throne,

With the strong energy of fear imprest,
Thee, SON OF HEAV'N! his iron hands arrest:
Grasp not alone the common joys of life,
But ev'n the brightest gem, THY LOVING WIFE:
Inhuman monster! smiling at the smart,
That nature shot thro' each united heart.
BEHOLD THE SCENE, the piercing scene appears!
Imagination drops a pitying tear.
Bereft of thee, thy tender partner pines,
Thinks of thy state, and dangers new divines:
'Till in her bosom black despair conceives,
Nor beam of hope the pungent pain relieves;
Tho' thy misfortunes all her efforts claim,
The hand of nature bears upon her frame:
Feeble, and unassisted, hear her cry,
" *For thee, O husband! 'Tis for thee I die!*"
The martyr falls—Angelic guides convey
The spirit to the climes of endless day.
Ah! now the cruel tidings reach thine ear,
Thy dauntless courage melts into a tear:
Thy joints relax, thy fearful face grows wan,
And all the stoic softens into man:
For one soft moment other cares resign'd,
Ev'n LIBERTY, her image fills thy mind;
Yet in the cause thy soul unmov'd remains,
And from th' OPPRESSOR'S ROD new vigour gains.
How great thy sufferings! how amazing great!
Thy patience future poets shall relate!
Man shall record with gratitude thy name,
The winds from pole to pole shall waft thy fame.
And (if the Muse her object may pursue,
And set futurity to mortal view;)
Ere thou rejoicing yield'st thy fleeting breath,
Thy wife to follow thro' the paths of death;
FREEDOM SHALL REIGN! from earth thou shalt arise;
And bear the tidings to th' impatient skies.

And will ye deign to hear my mean applause,
Ye friends of man, and pillars of the cause!
Who, firm as rocks, amid the storm have stood,
And dar'd all dangers for the public good;
Ye, who with HARDY NOW are doom'd to feel
The lawless vengeance of ambitious zeal!
How would my heart with gen'rous rapture glow,
Could my weak strain alleviate your woe;
Inspire some noble bosom to a deed,
Humanity and Nature's dictates plead,
TO PITY YOUR MISFORTUNES; and impart
His needful succour:—Every feeling heart,
Eager must yield the strongest aid it can,
To *prop* the *cause* of *God*, of *Angel*, and of *Man!*

A Friend to the distressed Patriots.

One would have naturally supposed that the wretches, who had so long amused themselves by sporting with the feelings of this unfortunate couple, would have been disarmed of their malignity, by the death of a much injured and amiable woman, and would have stopped in the midst of their shameful career; but the diabolical rancour of their minds was not to be thus satisfied. It is scarcely credible, that in a country celebrated for its humanity and liberality, such conduct should have been still pursued; yet so it was; for on the very day, or the day but one after the death of Mrs. Hardy, calumnious paragraphs appeared in the TIMES NEWSPAPER.

Hardy's place of confinement was a small room above the western gate of the Tower. Mr. Thelwall's room was next, and Mr. Tooke's below. Here he remained for about ten or twelve days after the mournful event already narrated, without taking his accustomed walks—for the prisoners had been permitted to walk on the ramparts and parade some hours each day, for some time before—in a state of mind impossible for tongue or pen to describe, deprived of the faithful and beloved partner of his bosom, the participator of all his joys, and the kind and tender alleviator of all his sorrows; and without that variety of objects and occupations which divert the minds of men in Society, in a certain measure, from continually brooding over their afflictions; his mental sufferings must have been extreme. At length his fellow prisoners not meeting him in their daily rounds, his friend, Mr. Tooke, found means, privately, of advising him not to confine himself so closely, but to walk out and meet his friends in the different rendezvous which they had appointed; that, by seeing, and privately conversing with them, it might relieve his spirits, and enable him, with more fortitude, to meet the tremendous trial which awaited him; for, about this time, there were some hints in the public papers that they were to be tried for High Treason.

The Special Commission of Oyer and Terminer, for enquiring into, and hearing and determining of all High Treasons, and misprison of Treason, in compassing or imagining the death of the King, &c. was dated the 10th of September, 1794. The volume of written evidence was so enormous, that the Attorney General was upwards of nine hours in opening the case to the Jury. Never was such a host of Crown Lawyers employed against any person tried for High Treason; and they certainly did justice to their employers, for they strained every nerve, in order to criminate their intended victim. The whole weight of the arm of power was employed to crush him; for if his ruin could be once accomplished, the other eleven who were in the indictment with him, were reckoned upon as an easy sacrifice.

It appears that the Government felt so confident of a conviction, that they had prepared eight hundred warrants, three hundred of which were actually signed, in order to be ready to be executed that very night and the next morning, in case a verdict of guilty were returned. Who the persons thus marked for destruction were, Hardy did not learn, but he is compelled to believe the authority upon which he states the damning fact. No means, however unjustifiable, were spared, that could effect his ruin. Letters written by others to different persons, without his knowledge or consent, and which he had never seen or heard of, until they were produced in Court, were attempted to be read in evidence against him, and one of that description was actually admitted.

The following papers, which he found means of conveying privately to his brother-in-law, Mr. Walne, two days previously to his removal from the Tower, will shew what desperate means Hardy's blood thirsty enemies had recourse to, in order, if possible, to take away his life, so plainly, that it needs no comment.

" On Thursday last, Mr. Kinghorn, the Gentleman Gaoler, and Underwood, a Warder, came into my room. Mr. Kinghorn seemed much agitated, and asked me to step with him to the Governor's, where he said a gentleman was waiting, who wished to speak with me. I inquired who it was, and what it was about? Mr. Kinghorn replied, that he did not know, but believed it to be something about subpœnas. Not suspecting that a trap had been laid for me, I went readily with him, and two Warders, to the Governor's house on the parade. In the dining-room into which I was shewn, one of the clerks of Mr. White, Solicitor to the Treasury, was sitting alone. When we entered, he arose from his seat, with what might be taken for an innocent smile on his countenance, and, addressing his discourse to me, said, ' Mr. Hardy, Mr. White omitted to inform you, when he delivered the indictment, that your Solicitor, by applying at the Crown Office, may have subpœnas for your witnesses without any expense to you.' All that I said in reply was, very well and with a low bow returned with the Gaoler and the two Warders, in order to return to my room. In my way back I met Mr. Clarkson, my Solicitor, and told him where I had been, and what orders I had to give him. He replied that he had received a letter from Mr. White, the day before, to the same purport. While we were standing together talking, another of Mr. White's clerks, with a woman on his arm, came close up to us, and the female stared very hard at me. They walked on a few paces, then returned, and stared as before. I then recollected having seen the same couple standing opposite the Governor's door, apparently watching me as I came out. These two clerks were with White when he delivered the indictment; and this is the Miss Jane Partridge, of Nottingham, one of the witnesses for the Crown. They have had recourse to this artifice, to give her an opportunity of identifying my person. Before I had returned to my room five minutes, the same man whom I saw at the Governor's house came up to Thelwall, who is in the next room to me, and told him the same he had told me. This conduct caused some suspicion. Why should there have been such parade about my going to the Governor's, and yet the same message be delivered to Thelwall in his own room? We have enquired, and find that no such message has been sent to any of the other prisoners. There must, therefore, be some design in it.

"The mystery has been unfolded. Mr. Joyce, of Essex Street, informs us, that this woman has been brought to the Tower on purpose to see me; and it seems she is satisfied that I am the person who travelled with her from Nottingham to London, in the stage coach, about two years ago; and what she is to swear to is this: that I said to her in the coach that I would no more mind cutting off the King's head than I would shaving myself. Take particular notice of this woman; if she swears to such words, she perjures herself, for I never was at Nottingham in my life, nor farther north from London, by land, than Hampstead or Highgate."

Tower, 20th October, 1794.

How to counteract the evidence of this very wicked, or very much mistaken woman, was a very material point, and to be immediately considered. The circumstance was, without delay, communicated to the friends of the prisoners, and they set actively to work, and found persons who could prove satisfactorily that Hardy was not out of London one whole day, for more than a year before, and after the time she was to swear to.

The hand of Providence is evident in the manner in which the testimony that Jane Partridge was to give was discovered. What evidence the other witnesses for the Crown were to give, had been pretty well ascertained; but to what circumstance she was to bear witness, puzzled the friends of the prisoners. It happened, that the same evening she had been at the Tower to see Hardy, she drank tea with a party of young ladies, among whom there chanced to be the sister of Mr. Wardle, one of those in the indictment, but not in custody. Here Miss Wardle learnt the nature of Jane Partridge's evidence, and immediately communicated the circumstance to Mr. Joyce, of Essex Street, who went instantly to the Tower, and informed Hardy. Thus, great danger was averted; for had nothing been known of the nature of her evidence before her coming into Court, it would then be difficult to rebut it: there would be no witnesses prepared to prove that Hardy had not been at Nottingham, and, consequently, could not have travelled with Jane Partridge from that town to London. When the trial came on, and she was ordered into Court, she fainted in the room where the Crown witnesses were. When recovered, she was again called in, and again fainted. Whether the managers of the prosecution thought it best to dispense with her evidence, from a fear of its containing some fatal self-contradictions, or whether they found it impossible, from the effect that conscious guilt had upon her, to obtain that evidence, we know not; but she was no more called. It is clear, however, were her nerves as strong as her heart, and those of her employers were corrupt and wicked, that she would have ventured her eternal salvation by trying, falsely, to swear away the life of a man whom she had never seen, until she went to the Tower for that purpose.

It is to be hoped she lived to repent of her iniquity. If she is still living, it may be some consolation to her mind to know, that the man whom she would have destroyed forgives her.

A full report of the trial is already before the public. It lasted *nine days*, on the last of which, after the fullest investigation that ever took place in this or any other country, Hardy was pronounced " NOT GUILTY,"* by the unanimous voice of as respectable a jury as ever was empannelled. A jury, which, with unremitting patience, underwent a fatigue and confinement unparallelled in the annals of our courts of justice. A jury, on whose awful voice depended the liberties of eleven millions of their fellow citizens. A jury, whose integrity established on a firm basis the first and most important pillar of the English Constitution,—THE TRIAL BY JURY, which had been greatly on the decline, and much tampered with, for some time before, and thereby entitled

---

* On hearing of the acquittal of Hardy, John M'Creery, the printer and poet, wrote the following lines:—

> Twelve true hearted men held the balance of fate,
> While these Shylocks were whetting the knife:
> Of th' existence of thousands they lengthened the date—
> Their VERDICT was FREEDOM and LIFE.

themselves to the grateful acknowledgments and applause, both of the present and of future generations.

Having thus seen the subject of our Memoir delivered by twelve honest men from the power of his merciless persecutors, it will not, we trust, be deemed altogether foreign to our purpose to say a few words respecting the others who were in the same indictment with him.

Mr. Tooke was the subject of vindictive persecution and prosecution, because he had been from early life an ardent supporter of the rights of his fellow men. His talents were of the first order, and he distinguished himself as an active and formidable champion in favour of, what was then called, *Wilkes and liberty*. On that occasion his oratory and writings were equally admired, for their energy, perspicuity, independence, and constitutional spirit.

In spite of the oppressions and violence of the Court, Mr. Wilkes, in 1768, became a candidate for the county of Middlesex. On that occasion, Mr. Horne rode throughout the whole county, canvassing for him, which was the principal cause of his being elected. Mr. Horne was brought to the bar of the House of Commons, for a letter signed "*Strike but Hear*," published in The Public Advertizer, 14th of February, 1774, in favour of a petition of W. Tooke, Esq. respecting the enclosing of an estate. Shortly afterwards, by virtue of an Act of Parliament, he took the name of Tooke, at the desire of the same gentleman, who adopted him, and left him that estate which he had preserved from being swallowed up to satisfy the cormorant appetite of the law, at a time when he expected no other advantage from such essential services, than the conscious satisfaction of having procured justice to be done to a fellow citizen, about to be injured under the mask of legal forms. It is gratifying to see such eminent virtue and talent meet with their well merited reward, in such very unequivocal testimony of friendship and gratitude, as was thus given by Mr. Tooke to Mr. Horne, now Horne Tooke.

Mr. Tooke's trial lasted six, Thelwall's four days; and the prosecutors, finding they could not obtain a conviction, declined proceeding with the trials of the other nine.

Mr. John Thelwall is well known, and highly esteemed as a public lecturer on politics, classical literature, and general education, in London, and various other parts of England and Scotland. He is also the author of many valuable works in prose and verse, and still lives highly and deservedly respected by a great number of his countrymen.

Stewart Kyd was an eminent barrister, author of a great law work, and of several political productions.

Augustus Bonney, an attorney of great repute.

Jeremiah Joyce, a man of great worth, and highly esteemed by all who knew him; was some years in the family of the late Earl Stanhope, as tutor to his sons. He was the author of several excellent sermons, some political tracts, and various valuable works on the arts and sciences.

Thomas Holcroft, a celebrated novelist, dramatic writer, and traveller.

The other five were John Richter, Thomas Wardle, Matthew Moore, Richard Hodgson, and John Baxter: all excellent men, and sincere and active promoters of Parliamentary Reform.

As severe sufferers in the same great cause, it is to be hoped that a very brief notice of those gentlemen who were tried at Edinburgh, will not be deemed out of place here. They were all men of education and talents, and their only crime was being sincere in a cause from which Mr. Pitt had become an apostate. The proceedings against them in the Court of Justiciary of Scotland, excited universal odium throughout the country, and were execrated in terms of indignation by several Members of both Houses of Parliament.

Skirving and Gerald did not live long after their arrival at Botany Bay. Palmer, and another, purchased a vessel which had been a prize taken into Botany Bay, and intended coming home in her; but she was very leaky, and they were obliged to put into, as it happened, the very port to which the vessel belonged, where she was re-seized with her cargo, consisting of poor Palmer's whole property. Here all his sufferings closed soon after.

Mr. Margarot was a man of a strong philosophical understanding, ready wit, undaunted courage, and incorruptible integrity. He was the only one, of the five, who returned to his native country. He died about fifteen years ago.

Mr. Thomas Muir, younger, of Hunter's Hill, was a man animated by strong enthusiasm, insomuch that even some Reformers blamed him for the indiscretion of his zeal; but it must be admitted that the zeal that is required to reform a system of abuses, ought to be intense, and should obtain forgiveness for any slight excesses it may run into. The following letter, written by Hardy to a friend, with a print of Muir, and containing quotations from his address to the Jury, and the Lord Justice Clerk, will clearly evince the rectitude of his intentions, and that he did not think his punishment, by any means, an ignominy.

"DEAR SIR,

I was very much gratified when you informed me, the other day, that you had in your possession a box of manuscripts, letters, and papers, of that excellent man, the late Thomas Muir, who was cruelly sentenced by the Court of Justiciary, of Edinburgh, on the 31st of August, 1793, to 14 years transportation, to the inhospitable shore of Botany Bay. For what? What was his crime? Strange to tell—for a life of virtuous conduct up to that hour. Hear what he says to the Jury at the close of his celebrated defence. " This is now, perhaps, the last time that I shall address my country. I have explored the tenor of my past life. Nothing shall tear me from the record of my departed days. From my infancy to this moment, I have devoted myself to the cause of the people. It is a good cause; it shall ultimately prevail; it shall finally triumph. Say then, openly, in your verdict, if you do condemn me, which I presume you will not, that it is to this cause alone, and not for those vain and wretched pretexts stated in the indictment, intended only to colour and disguise the real motives of my accusation. Weigh well the verdict you are to pronounce. As for me, I am careless and indifferent to my fate. I can look danger, I can look death in the face, for I am shielded by the consciousness of my own rectitude. Nothing can deprive me of the resolution of the past. Nothing can destroy my inward peace of mind, arising from the remembrance of having done my duty."

After the Judge had delivered the sentence, Mr. Muir rose, and said:—" *My Lord Justice Clerk, I have only a few words to say. I shall not animadvert on the severity or the leniency of my sentence. Were I to be led this moment from the bar to the scaffold, I should feel the same calmness and serenity which I now do. My mind tells me, that I have acted agreeably to my conscience, and that I have engaged in a good—a just and a glorious cause, a cause which sooner or later must, and will prevail; and, by a timely reform, save this country from destruction.*"

With this I send a print of Thomas Muir for your acceptance.

When the Surprise transport was lying off Portsmouth, at Motherbank, in which these persecuted patriots, *Muir, Palmer, Margarot,* and *Skirving,* were sent to Botany Bay, I was on board of her at the time, and saw Mr. Banks, who was an eminent statuary, take a cast from Muir's face, from which he afterwards made a bust, and from which the present engraving is taken. It is a good likeness.

Accept, Dear Sir, the best wishes of
THOMAS HARDY."

3rd March, 1821.
To Mr. Witherspoon, Cheapside.

Muir escaped from Botany Bay, on board a South Sea Whaler; was shipwrecked on the coast of South America, and after a variety of hardships reached the Havannah. His misfortunes did not end here. He took a passage on board of a Spanish vessel for Europe; and this country being at that time at war with Spain, they were attacked by a British frigate, off Cadiz. In this rencounter a splinter struck Muir on the cheek, part of which it carried away, and destroyed the sight of one of his eyes. The Spanish vessel was boarded, and he was recognized, while lying among the wounded, by a British officer, as an old acquaintance, and this circumstance enabled him to get to Spain. At the invitation of the National Convention, he went soon afterwards to France, where the Government granted him a pension, which he enjoyed until his death.

The particulars of his eventful life have been recently published.

It was a most fortunate circumstance that the public prosecutor made choice of Hardy as the first victim to be sacrificed to ministerial vengeance. Had the friends of Reform themselves the election, a better could not have been made. Perhaps there never was a man, in any country, brought to the bar of a Court of Justice, for an imputed great crime, who could find so many respectable and creditable persons to testify to the uniform goodness of his private and moral character. So numerous, indeed, were they, that his learned, eloquent, and excellent counsel, Erskine, and Gibbs, deemed it unnecessary to bring any thing like the whole of them forward.

During the whole of the trial, the conscious rectitude of his own heart shone conspicuously through that index of the mind, the face. There the court, the jury, the learned bar, and the anxious and highly interested auditory, might plainly read the integrity of the honest man; the inflexible firmness of the patriot, proud of having been called to answer, even with his life, for his exertions in the cause of freedom; for his efforts to obtain for himself, and fellow countrymen, a restoration of those inestimable rights which had raised the British name to that pre-eminence it had so long held among surrounding nations, and the abandoning of which would have degraded it to a level with the most slavish of them.

The room in which he was confined in Newgate, during his trial, was in the inner prison, and he had, every morning, to walk through the yard in which the felons were allowed to walk. They were heavily ironed, some with single, and some with double fetters. They were upon each side, and as he walked through the middle, he found that even men of that description could distinguish between a man suffering for the assertion of honest principles, and those suffering for a breach of those moral restraints that bind society together.

They all expressed their good wishes towards him, in one way or other, and congratulated him on his good spirits.

When he passed the room in which Mr. Kyd was confined, every morning, they shook hands through the iron grating. On the third day, he said cheerfully to Kyd, " Now, Kyd, this day, death or liberty;" but he was mistaken, for his persecutors protracted the struggle as long as they had any hopes of success.

Mr. Ridgway, Mr. Symonds, and others, were confined on the State side of the prison for libels, or, in other words, for publishing the truth. As he passed here every morning, on his way to the court, they crowded to the gate, anxious to shake hands with him, and to express their good wishes. One morning as he passed the gate in high spirits, he said to Ridgway, " We are going to have another long spell at it to-day." On the Sunday before the trial finished, as he was walking in the yard with Mr. Kyd, and some others of his fellow prisoners, Mr. Kirby, the Keeper of Newgate, asked him if he would like to see the condemned cells—he accepted the invitation, without any hesitation, and went along with Kirby, accompanied by his friend Kyd. The poor unfortunate men were then walking in a small yard opposite the doors of their melancholy dwellings; consequently the cells were empty. What conversation took place, or what remarks were made by Hardy on those horrible places, it is unnecessary to repeat; but we may conceive that the sight was not very pleasing to a man in his situation, when it was uncertain whether he might not be lodged in one of them himself in two or three days.

Immediately on the words " NOT GUILTY" being pronounced by the foreman of the worthy jury, the Sessions House, where the court sat, was almost rent with loud and reiterated shouts of applause. The vast multitude that were waiting anxiously without, caught the joyful sound, and like an electric shock, or the rapidity of lightning, the glad tidings spread through the whole town, and were conveyed much quicker than the regular post could travel, to the most distant parts of the island, where all ranks of people were anxiously awaiting the result of the trial.

After these extraordinary effusions of joy had a little

abated in the court, Mr. Kirby, the Gaoler, advised Hardy to go through the prison to the debtor's door, where a coach was in readiness to convey him, according to his directions, to the house of his brother-in-law, Mr. Walne, in Lancaster Court, in the Strand; for he had no house of his own left to go to, nor family to welcome him home. Although he went into the coach as privately as possible, and drove down Snow Hill, yet he was observed by some persons, and the circumstance was announced to the multitude, who turned it into another direction, drove it along Fleet Market; and when they came to the end of Fleet Street, the concourse of people was very great, though it was a bleak rainy afternoon in the gloomy month of November. Here they stopped the coach, took out the horses, and drew it along Fleet Street, the Strand, Pall-Mall, St. James's Street, Piccadilly, the Haymarket, and back again to Lancaster Court, where he alighted. He addressed the people from the window in a short speech, after which they gave three cheers, and quietly dispersed, leaving him to enjoy the evening with some particular friends, among whom were the Rev. Dr. Bogue, and Rev. James Steven. During the procession, the people frequently stopped, and shouted at different places, such as Charing Cross, Carleton House, and St. James's Palace. At No. 9, Piccadilly, his former comfortable habitation, they stopped a few minutes in *solemn silence.*

The joy that appeared in every countenance of the vast multitudes of people who thronged the windows of the houses, in the streets through which the procession passed, was truly gratifying. In fact, the general joy that the acquittal of Hardy diffused throughout the country, was never exceeded, perhaps never equalled. It was heartfelt and extensive; the triumph of freedom was complete over those who wished to crush it at one blow; and every liberal-minded man felt himself, and not without reason, as if unexpectedly relieved from some terrible impending danger.

Shortly after a public meeting, at which Earl Stanhope presided, was held at the Crown and Anchor, to celebrate the result of the State Trials. All parts of the house were filled, and it was calculated that the assemblage consisted of no fewer than a thousand persons. This meeting was addressed by the noble chairman, by Sheridan, and other gentlemen, with animation and effect; and the friends of Parliamentary Reform have met annually on the 5th of November, to commemorate the acquittal of Thomas Hardy from a charge of High Treason, on the same day of the month, 1794. On these occasions it is expected, when a gentleman's health is drank, that, on returning thanks, he will make a speech; but Hardy, not being an orator, has, of late years, previously committed to paper what he had to say on his health being drank. Three such addresses, with their dates, will be placed at the end of this sketch, and in which will be found an interesting account of some circumstances relating to the London Corresponding Society, not mentioned in the Memoir.

We shall close the political part of this Memoir with the following address to the jury, the counsel, and his friends in general; and we hope that the reader, who has thus far accompanied us, will find it consistent with the proper feeling evinced by Hardy throughout the whole of his imprisonment and trial. It was published in all the Newspapers of the time.

ADDRESS TO THE PUBLIC.

"WITH a heart overflowing with gratitude, I now sit down to the most pleasing task which I have experienced in the course of my life. Little did I imagine that the public efforts I have made, in support of that cause which I deemed it my duty to promote to the utmost of my power, would have excited, in so great a degree, the most lively emotions of affectionate regard in the bosoms of thousands to whom I am unknown, but by name.—But so it has happened, and I feel myself labouring under a weight of obligations, which I am ardently anxious to discharge, as far as my ability will permit.

" Untutored in any language but that of truth, I proceed, without fear of the attack either of prejudice or malevolence, to pay the debt I owe, as far as I am able.

" To MR. ERSKINE and MR. GIBBS, the two learned Counsel appointed for my defence, I beg permission, in this public manner, to return my best and warmest acknowledgments.—Any words in my power to use, would fall far short of expressing what they TRULY DESERVE, and what I REALLY FEEL they deserve. I have, however, this animating reflection in my mind, that every defect in my powers of expression to do them justice, is abundantly compensated by the force and eloquence of their own respective exertions, and that their transcendant talents and integrity cannot fail to stand recorded, not only on the minds of the present race, but will receive additional lustre in every progressive movement their names shall make through the progress of time.

" TO THAT PUBLIC, whose servant I have always been proud to acknowledge myself, I am equally at a loss for words to express the grateful sensations of my heart.—The feeling manner in which they have sympathized in my sufferings, while it gives a delight to my heart which no language can describe, almost disables me, from the overflowings of that source of sensibility, to perform my duty;—but the softness of nature gives way to the impetus of gratitude, and I beg leave to say to a generous public,

BE PLEASED TO ACCEPT MY THANKS.

" Acquitted by the unanimous voice of a jury of my country, from the charge of a crime at which my soul revolts, and my nature shudders, I find it impossible to express my gratitude to THEM in any degree adequate to what I feel. I must, therefore, intreat them for a moment to suppose themselves in my situation, and CONCEIVE what they would have said to me, had I, in similar circumstances, been their arbiter, and given the same decision in their behalf. I have no doubt but, in the consciousness of the rectitude of their own hearts, they feel a far greater reward than any in the power of mortal man to bestow;—but what I can I will:—I SINCERELY AND FERVENTLY THANK THEM.

"Small, indeed, is the return for the preservation of life and honour;—it is only the grateful effusions of a plain and poor man, but it comes warm from the heart, and, like the widow's mite, is ALL I HAVE TO GIVE.

"Restored to my friends and country after an absence of several months, in the course of which, all my family have descended into the peaceful tomb, I find my business ruined, and I have the world to begin again. I therefore take this opportunity of informing my friends, in particular, and the public in general, that I intend to resume my occupation, and to support myself as heretofore, by honest industry. I have not yet been able to find an eligible situation for opening a shop; but as soon as I can accomplish that object, I shall take the liberty of making it known, and have no doubt of receiving that encouragement and support which injured innocence never yet has failed to obtain in this generous and liberal island.

" THOMAS HARDY."

Lancaster Court, Strand,
  Nov. 11, 1794.

It has already been mentioned that Hardy had many flattering offers made to him, if he would go and settle in America,* and it is no wonder, on his acquittal, finding

---

* When Mr. Adams, the first Ambassador from the United States, was in this country, his son-in-law, Col. Smith, was his private Secretary. With that gentleman Hardy was very intimate, and supplied him with boots and shoes while he remained in England. Colonel Smith held out great encouragement to him if he would go and carry on his business in America. Hardy called on him one day, at the beginning of the London Corresponding Society, and shewed him the first Address, with which he

himself pennyless, his whole property having been expended in defending himself from the base charges exhibited against him, and his trade totally ruined, in consequence of his imprisonment, that he should have formed a resolution of bidding an everlasting adieu to a country where he had been thus maltreated : to a country where he had been so incurably wounded in his dearest affections; where he saw the most exalted virtues treated as the greatest crimes; where he had been persecuted to the imminent danger of his life, for what he himself, and all such as he could consider upright men, deemed his *virtuous* efforts, to restore to his fellow countrymen the inestimable blessing of a FREE PARLIAMENT, fairly chosen by the people. For these reasons, and they were sufficiently weighty, he finally determined to expatriate himself; but all human intentions must yield to the overruling power of the Omnipotent, who, in his wisdom, thought fit it should be otherwise. Though moneyless, he was not friendless; for, in fact, his friends were numerous, and some of them were sanguine in their hopes that, if he would recommence business in London, he would soon realize an independent fortune, which they said would prove some recompense, though an inadequate one, for all his wrongs and sufferings. He suffered himself, therefore, to be persuaded; altered his resolution, and recommenced business, in Tavistock Street, Covent Garden, on the 29th of November, 1794.

The public were certainly much interested in his favour; and the orders which he received, for the first two weeks, employed himself, and another man, merely to take measure, and to enter them in the book. Many paid for their

---

was well pleased, and, for his encouragement, said to Hardy, " Hardy, the Government will hang you." Though this prophecy was afterwards too near being fulfilled, yet he still lives a monument of the excellence of the TRIAL BY JURY.

orders at the time of giving them; some ordered two pair of shoes, and paid a guinea, and a few paid a guinea for one pair; and these the newspapers magnified to a thousand, at a guinea a pair. Multitudes of people, of all ranks and sexes, in carriages, and on foot, came to congratulate him; and crowds of persons were continually collected about the door and the windows, out of curiosity to see him. The shop, though large, was always full, from morning till night, and thus continued for, perhaps, two or three months, when it fell off gradually.

He employed, at first, six shopmen, to assist in carrying on the business; and it was, at one time, apparently encreasing; but when the public curiosity was satisfied, it began to decrease, and, at the end of six months, he found occasion for no more than two shopmen, and, within twelve months, for only one.

After his business had thus fallen to the level of ordinary trade, he found that, what with a large house, high rent, and high taxes, he was retrograding as rapidly as he had at first progressed. There were many unfounded reports spread abroad of the patronage which he received from a variety of quarters, which, though many wished and believed them true, operated greatly to his disadvantage. For instance, it was said, his landlord, the Duke of Bedford, had given him the house he inhabited rent free; that another nobleman had made him a present of five hundred pounds; and another had settled a hundred a year upon him. In consequence of these, and similar rumours, many gentlemen, who had intended to befriend him, thought it unnecessary, as they were led to believe he was already liberally provided for by the noble and the wealthy. They, therefore, turned their benevolence into other channels, and bestowed their favours upon others who they thought stood more in need of them—and, alas! many there were who had really need of support from the benevolent, at that time. So very injurious did these reports prove, that one of his leather merchants, in little more than a year, refused him credit. This was the son of the worthy Alderman Newman, who had so kindly called upon him the second day after his acquittal, and generously offered him credit, if he designed to go into business again, which kind offer he accepted. Another of his leather merchants actually served him with a copy of writ for a sum under ten pounds, which had been standing two months longer than the usual time of credit.

His journeymen, too, believing that he had greater profits on his goods than others had, struck for higher wages; but as they are a class of intelligent men, who can readily appreciate any question that is clearly stated to them, the following letter convinced them of the propriety of returning to their work at the same wages. The circumstance, however, which no doubt was owing to the unfounded stories which were afloat, was of some inconvenience to their employer, who was very busy at the time.

36, Tavistock Street, 24th April, 1795.

"FELLOW CITIZENS,

"It is with no small degree of pain, I now address you on a subject of considerable importance to me, and, I think I may add, of no less importance to you, as a body.

"I presume you are not unacquainted with the very peculiar situation I have been in since the beginning of last May. Six months of that time I was immured in a prison; and it must be fresh in the memory of every one of you the cruel persecution I suffered, and the probability there was of my being hurried from the prison to the scaffold; but thank God, it has been ordered otherwise, for the happiness of individuals, and the peace of the nation. Immediately on my regaining my liberty, I had some thoughts of leaving that country in which I had been so maltreated; but 1 found a great number of my friends, and friends also to the happiness of mankind, solicitous that I should remain in London, and go into business again, as I might be sure of a very extensive trade among those who felt for my situation, and were friendly to the cause I had espoused and suffered for. Accordingly, I was prevailed upon, took the house I now occupy; and, certainly, I have done a great deal of business within the last five months. Numbers employed me from real friendship; some came to see me from motives of curiosity, and gave orders, whom it is not likely I shall ever see again. Others, who came from the mere novelty of the thing, honestly told me that they did not mean to continue after the first orders, but to return again to their old shoemakers: very few have given me a second order. The whole of my customers are among what is called the middling and lower class of the people, who cannot, or who do not choose to give a high price for their shoes and boots. They must, also, have them strong, or, to use a common phrase, they must have a pennyworth for their penny. Not so the generality of the higher ranks of society, who care not how light their goods are, nor how high the prices. I have to inform you that my price for boots is £1. 8s., and for shoes 8s. 6d., some lower. When I opened this shop, I advanced the journeymen sixpence a pair on the shoes and boots above what I formerly used to give, which some of you may remember. Bootcloser's wages I also advanced.

" I have chosen to give you an open and candid statement of facts, which you, as a collective body, are to judge of betwixt me and those whom I formerly employed; and I think you have sufficient discernment to discover why I could not comply with the demand of my workmen.

" I ask no favour; I only wish for that which is just between man and man.—I have here to remark, that, according to my feeble ability, I have always been an enemy to all injustice and oppression, and for my opposition to them have suffered persecution; but I am still determined, as far as I can, to resist injustice or oppression, from whatever quarter they may be attempted, whether by my declared enemies, or my professed friends, though I should fall in the conflict.

"These few hasty thoughts I leave to your deliberation; and if there is any thing which I have not stated of which you wish to be informed, I am ready to explain, or give every reasonable information in my power to any two or three intelligent men you may depute for that purpose. I conclude, with sincerely wishing you, and all mankind, health and fraternity.

" THOMAS HARDY."

To the Society of Journeymen
  Boot and Shoemakers.

Though this letter dispelled the delusion under which the journeymen had laboured, with respect to their employer's growing fortunes, yet others continued still in that delusion. Soon after the State Trials, in 1794, John Redman, Esq. of Hatton Garden, made a will, in which he put Hardy down for a legacy; but, in a subsequent one, made about four years afterwards, his name was omitted, for which no reason can be assigned, except that the testator, like many others, thought the bequest unnecessary. This is the more likely, as Mr. Redman, as long as he lived, continued to employ him as his shoemaker. A few days after that gentleman's death, Dr. Cooke called upon Hardy, in Fleet Street, and congratulated him upon the fortune that had been left him: though he did not then know but it might be true that such was the case, yet, having been amused with so many stories of great things, for some years past, he did not feel much elated at the intelligence. He merely thanked the Doctor for his good wishes, and observed, that if it was large it should be applied to benevolent purposes, and if small, it would assist him in carrying on his business, for he then had need of assistance—and if it should prove as unreal as the other gifts and legacies he had been promised, and said to have received, he could jog on his old way without it: for his happy temper enabled him to take all things very easy, whether adverse or prosperous. Another legacy, which *another gentleman* was reported to have left to him, turned out to be as unsubstantial as the last.

One disappointment, in the legacy way, is particularly worthy of remark. A gentleman, of large fortune, in Derbyshire, of the name of Kant, soon after the State Trials, in 1794, made his will, and in testimony of his approbation of the ability, patriotic exertions, and splendid eloquence, displayed by Mr. Erskine, in his defence of Hardy, bequeathed him an estate worth upwards of thirty thousand pounds. Hardy himself was, also, handsomely mentioned in the will, to which Mr. Kant afterwards added a codicil. He died about seven years afterwards, and his attorney came up to London with the will inclosed in a letter, written by the gentleman himself at the time of making it. After Mr. Erskine had read the letter, he asked the attorney if he had taken the proper legal steps to make the codicil valid. He replied, no: then said Mr. Erskine, "By God you have lost me the estate!" Mr. Erskine sent for Hardy a few days afterwards, told him what had happened, and said that the will was void, through the ignorance, or villainy, of a stupid country attorney. Thus ended the last of the legacies.

That the rumours which were afloat, respecting the generous and liberal support which Hardy was receiving from the wealthy friends of liberty, should have been so readily, and so generally believed, may seem somewhat strange; but the following letters will, perhaps, in a great measure, account for some, if not for all of them. There the nucleus will be seen; and we know that rumour, in its nature, very much resembles a snow-ball, which gathers fresh matter rapidly as it rolls along.

" FRIEND LAUDERDALE,

" I cannot help addressing you by that familiar and endearing title. You have boldly exerted yourself in defence of the rights, and done what you could to promote the happiness of the people, both in your place in the Senate, and on other public occasions, in opposition to an all-powerful and an all-devouring Oligarchy.—From such conduct, persevered in, you deserve the title of Friend to your country. When I have said this much, I am not sensible that I have said any thing more than the truth. Give me leave now to turn your attention to a few facts which concern myself, and which you have either forgotten, or are perhaps unacquainted with. Of some of those, however, I know you are not ignorant, and I think they cannot have escaped your memory.

" Upwards of two years ago, a few days after my acquittal from the charge of High Treason, Mr. Jaques, the coal merchant, called upon me with a message, to wait upon you the next evening. He told me, also, that he understood from you, that something handsome was to be done for me. This intelligence, no doubt, was very pleasing; especially from the quarter from which it came, and as my circumstances were then in such a state as required the assistance of friends. I readily embraced the flattering invitation; with a chearful heart I set off to wait upon you, and was soon admitted into the room where you, Colonel Maitland, and Dr. Moore,* were sitting. After some very friendly and familiar conversation about the trial, the treatment I met with during my confinement, the state of my mind during the trial, and my own opinion as to the event of it, with a variety of things, which were the common topics at that important period, important to me, at least. You then informed me that you, and several gentlemen, con-

* The father of the brave General Sir John Moore,

sidering me as a very much injured and persecuted man, had determined to present me with a sum of money, in order to assist me in beginning business again, (as a proof of their sincerity.) You told me, at the same time, that you had already in your hands for this purpose no less a sum than one hundred pounds, and that next day you were going down to the Duke of Bedford's, where you expected to make it considerably more, from him and his friends. You desired me to call upon you the next day but one, when you would return from Woburn, and you would inform me what success you had. When I was about to depart, Colonel Maitland said to you, that you might as well let Hardy have that hundred pounds now, but I replied, that I had no immediate use for it just at that time, and that, until I got a house and shop, it might remain in your hands.—It was so settled, and I took my leave. Agreeably to your appointment, I did call on the next day but one, but it was said you was not at home. *Your Butler*, with whom I was intimate, informed me that it was your desire that I should call in the evening; I did so, but was told that you was just gone out. I was desired to call again in the morning, and even then you was engaged, and could not be spoken with. I was told, however, that if I came again in the evening, about six or seven o'clock, you would then be at leisure. I did call, but, as usual, you could not be seen; you had got company—so from morning to night, and from night to morning, alternately, for several weeks, did I continue this fruitless pursuit, till I was quite ashamed of being so troublesome to the servants. I felt, too, that the trouble I myself had was too much to intitle me to suppose, that I would at last be successful, notwithstanding your friendly and unsolicited professions towards me. I, therefore, determined to call no more, though I should beg for my daily bread. This resolution I formed and kept. I heard no more about that business till some time, I think, in last January, excepting from a variety of people, both in London, and from different parts of the country, and even from Ireland, who were profuse in their congratulations, on the many civilities and marks of friendship, which they were told I had received from you and the Duke of Bedford, &c.

"Some time in January, 1796, to the best of my recollection, I accidentally met with you, in company with Mr. Grey, and Mr. Tierney, at the Crown and Anchor Tavern: I dare say you may recollect the circumstance. You left them, and took me aside, and asked me very kindly how I did, and told me to call upon you next morning, or any other time that was most convenient, as you had forty pounds in your hands for me—twenty that Earl Derby gave, and twenty that you meant to give yourself; and that if I did not see you, Mr. Bowmaker, (your Steward,) would account with me. You then left me, and joined the company of Mr. Grey, and Mr. Tierney again, and went up stairs to the Whig Club Meeting. Two days afterwards I called at your house in Leicester Square, but received the same sort of answer which I had been accustomed to receive before. You was not at home. I called many times for several weeks, but could not meet with either you or Mr. Bowmaker; till at last, either by accident, or convenience, I know not which, neither is it material to me, I met with Mr. Bowmaker, and stopped with him about two hours conversing, very dryly, indeed, about the public news, &c. expecting every moment when he would mention something of the business to me, as I understood from your Butler you had made your Steward acquainted with it. When I found that he took no notice of it, and my patience being by this time, exhausted, I mustered courage enough to inform him what you had told me at the Crown and Anchor Tavern. He replied that he did not know any thing of it, but that he should speak to you about it that same day, and desired me to call again the next morning. Agreeably to his appointment I called, expecting to meet with him, but he happened, also, not to be at home, but had informed the Butler that he had not an opportunity of speaking to his Lordship; but I was to call the next morning. Time after time was I put off with these sorts of answers, for several weeks, 'till at last I was told, (to save me the trouble of calling so frequently), that Mr. Bowmaker was going into the City, about two or three o'clock that same afternoon, and would call upon me as he passed.

"That answer, I assure you, was a considerable relief to me, for, at that period, time was a little more value to me than it is at present, or has been ever since; and as it left me without a pretence of again troubling you or your servants, I have ever since carefully avoided mentioning the subject.

"Various are the constructions which may be put upon the commencement, the progress, and the termination of this business, so far as you are individually concerned; I would really wish to put the most favourable construction upon it if I knew it; I cannot see how I can have deserved to be tantalized in the manner I have described, which is a literal statement of facts, of which you cannot be altogether ignorant. I have been buoyed up with the hope of friendship, and have found myself left in the possession of the name only; and the report of it throughout the nation, instead of being of service to me, has operated very materially to my injury. Many who I knew had designed to befriend me, hearing of your liberality, and that of others, were, in fact, induced to turn their civilities another way, concluding that a man who was so handsomely and powerfully supported by the rich and the noble, stood in no need of the countenance which their slender ability enabled them to bestow. One Nobleman, they were told, had given me a free house to live in—another had settled upon me a hundred a year for life—and a third had presented me with a purse of five hundred guineas; and a thousand stories, equally absurd, ridiculous, and improbable, were industriously spread abroad. Some people rejoiced at my good fortune, while others, of a different temper, were filled with envy at seeing fortune apparently smiling so abundantly upon me—and it was stated with confidence by all, that I should not have occasion to remain in business above two or three years; that I was making a fortune rapidly, &c. Sorry am I to be obliged to say, that the contrary with me is a lamentable truth.

"Your proffered kindness certainly was unexpected, and unmerited on my part; but being so handsomely offered, and, after a lapse of two years, remaining unperformed, it appears to me that I cannot be too presuming in considering myself to have a fair claim to some sort of explanation; without this, I must be led to suppose that since the first time you spoke to me, some particular part of my conduct has deprived me of that esteem which I had flattered myself I possessed in your mind, and put a stop to those liberal and generous exertions in my behalf, which you were good enough to think my unjust persecution demanded; or, perhaps, you may have been led into the same error as many others, by believing what is so confidently, though falsely asserted, that I had such an overflow of business, that it was of little use either to assist or employ me. If those *real* friends, who, amidst the foolish and ridiculous reports that are so industriously circulated, did assist and employ me, and continue still so to do, had argued in this way, it is not difficult to conceive where I would have been long ere now.

"Whatever may have been your motives respecting me, from first to last, I hope I shall stand excused for troubling you with the perusal of this long address. I have ruminated, for some time, upon the propriety of this measure, and it has been with the utmost reluctance that I at last resolved upon it. In carrying that resolution into effect, I conceive that I am doing a duty to myself, by endeavouring to procure an explanation of a conduct for which I cannot account; and, perhaps, it may ultimately turn out that I am doing justice to you at the same time; for I cannot allow myself to imagine, that the facts which I have stated, (which have hitherto been buried in my own breast,) can lay claim to the sanction of your name.

"THOMAS HARDY.

23rd January, 1797. " *36, Tavistock Street.*"
To the Earl of Lauderdale.

No notice was taken of this letter, until his Lordship was, two years afterwards, reminded of the circumstance, by the following letter.

" MY LORD,

" IT is by the desire and advice of some friends, to whom my situation and circumstances in life are no secret, and to whom I long since made known the promises, which, at different times, I have received from your Lordship, that I now address to you a few lines.

" I need not, I am sure, remind you, that when first you did me the favour of an interview, near four years ago, you assured me, in the presence of Dr. Moore, and Col. Maitland, that you had already received for me, from your friends, the sum of £100., in order to assist me in re-entering on my business; nor can there be occasion to say any thing respecting the second interview, when you told me that you had received £20. from the Earl of Derby for me. These sums, to you, are, no doubt, trifling, but to a person in my situation, struggling against difficulties, of which you can have no conception, they, (or either of them,) are of real moment.

" My friends have, therefore, urged me to recall these circumstances to your recollection, in the full persuasion that you will have the goodness, as speedily as may be, to direct your steward, or agent, to realise those expectations, which I was so confidently led to indulge from your promises. But if, (which I cannot well bring myself to believe,) I have been flattered with hopes of assistance, never to be afforded, or by assurances of sums of money, received for my use, which have never been subscribed, I hope it will not be reckoned too great a favour for me to expect, that the real state of the case may be fairly, and, at once, explained to me. I will only add, that I have formerly been told by Mr. Perry, who is supposed to be much in the secrets of those gentlemen with whom you act, that money had been raised for me; and that very lately, I could scarcely gain credit to my assertions, when being put into a situation, which obliged me to declare, that I had never received any assistance through your Lordship's hands."

" THOMAS HARDY.
" 161, *Fleet Street.*"

August 24, 1798.
To the Earl of Lauderdale.

On the 4th of September following, Hardy received *forty pounds, twenty from the Earl of Lauderdale himself,* and twenty from the Earl of Derby, accompanied by the following Note.

"*Edin., Saturday.*

"Sir,

"I have this day received yours; I have always forgot to send you £40., which, however, I now enclose you; except Lord Derby, I could collect from nobody; it is, therefore, £20. from him, and £20. from myself. I am very ill in bed, and can hardly write.

"Yours, &c. &c.

"LAUDERDALE.

"On reading your letter a second time, I see you say I had received £100. for you, in which you are completely wrong, £20. was the whole, and this, together with my own, you might have received at any time.

"Pray acknowledge the receipt."

On the receipt of this sum, Hardy wrote Notes of acknowledgment, of which the following are copies.

"My Lord,

"I RECEIVED your letter, enclosing a draft for £40., £20. was from the Earl of Derby. Accept my warmest thanks for your Lordship's kindness to me. Sincerely hoping that your health may be speedily restored, and that your country may long be benefited by your exertions in the cause of public liberty and happiness,

"I remain, with great respect,

"Your obliged and obedient servant,

"THOMAS HARDY.
"161, *Fleet Street.*"

September 7, 1798.
To the Earl of Lauderdale.

" MY LORD,

"HAVING received £20. from your Lordship, through the hands of the Earl of Lauderdale, I beg leave to offer you my most grateful acknowledgments for this act of kindness. Be assured, that while I have life, I can never forget the goodness of those gentlemen who have so generously stepped forward to assist me in sustaining the difficulties in which I was involved by a public prosecution. Hoping that my country may long enjoy your exertions for her liberty and happiness,

" I remain, with the greatest respect,

" Your much obliged and obedient servant,

" THOMAS HARDY.
" 161, *Fleet Street.*"

September 11, 1798.
To the Earl of Derby.

While upon pecuniary matters, it will be proper to insert here the following correspondence, which took place between THOMAS HARDY, The Right Honourable Henry Dundas, the Duke of Portland, and THE KING.

" SIR,

" ON the 12th of May, 1794, various effects of mine were seized, and carried away from my house, No. 9, Piccadilly, by a messenger, under a warrant, bearing your signature. I make this application to you, to demand their immediate restitution.

" THOMAS HARDY.
" 36, *Tavistock Street, Covent Garden.*
" *October* 12, 1796."

To the Right Hon. Henry Dundas.

" SIR,

" I REPEAT the demand which I made to you last week; namely, that you would restore to me immediately my property, which was seized in my house, No. 9, Piccadilly, on the 12th of May, 1794, by a warrant, bearing your signature.

"THOMAS HARDY.
"36, *Tavistock Street, Covent Garden.*"

October 22, 1796.
To the Right Hon. Henry Dundas.

"MR. DUNDAS has received Mr. Hardy's letter, which he has transmitted to the Secretary of State for the Home Department, to whom the consideration of the subject exclusively belongs.

"*Parliament Street, Oct.* 23, 1796."

To Mr. Hardy,
36, Tavistock Street.

"THOMAS Hardy learns, by a note from Henry Dundas, dated the 30th of October, 1796, that the Secretary of State for the Home Department is acquainted with the demand which he made, by two applications, to Henry Dundas, (supposing him to be Secretary of State for the Home Department,) for the restoration of the property seized from him in his house, No. 9, Piccadilly, on the 12th of May, 1794, by a warrant, signed, Henry Dundas. Thomas Hardy has waited above a fortnight since the last application, and he now demands, from the Duke of Portland, as Secretary of State for the Home Department, that the property seized, under the above mentioned warrant, be immediately restored.

"36, *Tavistock Street, Covent Garden.*
"*November* 8, 1796."

To His Grace the Duke of Portland, Secretary
of State for the Home Department.

TO THE KING IN COUNCIL.

"Sire,

"Your Ministers have bereaved me of my wife and my child;—they have attempted to take away my life, and, failing in their plots, they have done every thing in their power to destroy my good name in society.—After such accumulated wrongs, my present complaint may be thought unworthy of notice. There was, indeed, a time when I could have addressed you as a father—a husband—a man—I could have called on you, on the pledge of these relations, to pity my sufferings;—that time is past:—I ask now only for justice;—I petition the King for justice; for I am too poor to obtain it in his courts of law.—Your Ministers have robbed me of my property—it is now in their hands. It is not enough that I languished in a goal—that my small means were expended in my cause—that I was sent pennyless into the world.—Their malice was not contented—they withheld from me that which may appear trifling in your eyes, but is not so to a poor man. I have no other resource left, than to desire you, Sire, to command your Ministers to restore to me every thing which, by the warrant of the Secretary of State, was, on the 12th of May, 1794, taken from my house in Piccadilly.

"THOMAS HARDY.
"*36, Tavistock Street, Covent Garden.*
December 5, 1796.

"The King will perceive, by the subjoined correspondence between Thomas Hardy, Henry Dundas, and the Duke of Portland, that Thomas Hardy refrained from troubling the King till the necessity of the case could amply plead in his justification."

Having received no answer to this last application, he made several unsuccessful attempts to bring the business before Parliament. His want of success, in these attempts, was owing to the circumstance of Mr. Fox, and the other distinguished Members of the Opposition, having *withdrawn* from the House of Commons, which, according to the principles of our Constitution, ought, in a peculiar manner, to represent the people—as finding it in vain to oppose their integrity and splendid talents to the strong tide of corruption. He, therefore, gave up all hopes of redress. Such was the result of the above correspondence, if correspondence that can be called, where the greater number of one party's letters are never answered by the other.

As a last resort, he published the whole correspondence, on the 13th of November, 1797, in the London Courier newspaper, that the public might see that no man's property nor person were safe, even in his own house, from the rapacity and lawless violence of men armed with usurped power. He was plundered of property of considerable value, among other things, of his pocket book, as already mentioned, which, with other papers, contained two inland bills of exchange: one of them was on J. Callender, for £136.; the other, for £60., was accepted by G. Sutton, Esq. M.P. and became due on the 25th of January, 1794. When it was presented for payment, he did not honour it; but declared that " he had not a sixpence to take it up with, and should not be in possession of money until June, when the Parliament would be prorogued!!" About a week afterwards, the bill was again presented, and the same answer returned; it was then that Hardy threatened to compel payment, to which Sutton's reply was, " You cannot arrest me; I am a Member of Parliament!!" Hardy then saw that there was no alternative but to wait until June, when the *Honourable Gentleman* should have received his half yearly salary, for voting on all questions as the Minister directed him: but before June, (12th May,) he and the bills were both secured, by the warrant of the Secretary of the State; and from that day to this he has not seen the bills, nor any other part of the property he had been robbed of; nor has G. Sutton had the honesty to pay his bill that was then due.* This is but a small sample of the robberies committed by Mr. Pitt's Administration.

While speaking of robberies, sanctioned by legal sophistry, though not exactly in chronological order, this may not be an improper place to mention two instances in which Hardy was robbed without that sanction. A short time after his arrival in London, some thieves broke into his room, stole his clothes, and left him almost naked; but being then a single man, he soon procured more by his industry, and forgot his loss. The next instance was a little more serious: the first Christmas after he was married, the same description of lawless people broke into his house, when he and Mrs. Hardy were visiting at a friend's house, took all their clothes, and almost stripped the shop of its contents of boots and shoes. He was thankful that they had left the bed and clothes behind. By persevering industry he overcame this loss also; and after struggling some years against wind and tide, to use a seaman's phrase, he had the harbour of prosperity full in view, when he was attacked by more powerful *Buccaneers*;

---

* The reader will recollect that this was written in 1796. On Mr. Margarot's departure for Botany Bay, where he was sent, it cannot be too often repeated, for fourteen years, by the arbitrary and unjust sentence of the Court of Justiciary, he left the two bills with Hardy; and, on his return, after seventeen years absence, he applied to Mr. Litchfield, Secretary to the Treasury, for the two bills, or payment for them. After a good deal of searching and enquiries, they could not be found; and Mr. Margarot insisted on payment, or else he would lay his case before Parliament. Probably Government considered it better to pay the money privately, than to bring so disagreeable and disgraceful a subject, then partially forgotten, again before the public. Be that as it may, Margarot got his money from Government.

or, to drop the metaphor, when he was plundered by thieves of a worse description, under the authority of GEORGE THE THIRD'S PRIVY COUNCIL!

When his property was completely destroyed, his person nearly sacrificed to their wicked designs, and he was again sent into the world almost as bare as he came into it, without a home, and without the dear partner of his joys and sorrows to welcome him, and to rejoice in his escape from a cruel, sanguinary, and unjust prosecution. This is repetition, but the wrongs which have called it forth were repeated; and, surely, the magnitude of those wrongs may well plead an excuse for it.

It is already manifest, that the stories so commonly believed of the Eldorado that was pouring in upon him in Tavistock Street, were entirely without foundation. These rumours gave rise, however, to one thing which grieved him very much, because it was impossible for him to act according to his inclination in respect to it. He received many letters and petitions from poor distressed people, to which it was out of his power, in all instances, to attend. To many of the most distressing he did attend, but it was painful to his mind to be obliged to dismiss others with only his good wishes, which was like saying to them, in the language of Scripture, " Be ye warmed, and be ye filled."

But the public delusion did not confine itself to pecuniary matters alone. Hardy was exalted, by public credulity, to a level with the first practitioners of the law, and, strange as it may appear, many persons, and among them, some men of learning and ability, applied to him for the solution of some very knotty perplexities, and intricate points of law; conceiving, no doubt, that as he had passed unhurt through such an ordeal, he must be a very clever fellow. Some of them did not know that he was only a shoemaker, and incapable of giving an opinion on any point of law. To all that applied to him about law, his uniform advice was, not to go to law upon any account, when it was possible to avoid it.

Whatever difficulties he had to struggle with, during the latter part of his time in Tavistock Street, he did not, for some time, communicate to any of his friends, otherwise they would have readily relieved him. Indeed, had his particular friends given ear to the absurd stories that were in circulation, and, in consequence, neglected to support him with their custom, he would have found himself, at the end of two years, worse off than ever; but, fortunately for him, they were too much of matter of fact men to be so misled. He had many real friends, even among those who differed widely from him in political opinions. These candidly told him, that they did not employ him on account of his politics, but because they thought him a persecuted and injured man. He refused money, at the time of his recommencing business, out of delicacy, from gentlemen, who, no doubt, offered it generously and freely. Such refusals, he had afterwards reason to believe, were construed to his disadvantage. Towards these gentlemen, however, he felt, and confessed his gratitude, as much as if he had availed himself of their favours.

A gentleman in Fish Street Hill, whose name we are not at liberty to mention, sent his son, two or three days after Hardy had settled in Tavistock Street, with ten guineas, saying that it might be useful to him in his then circumstances, and that he would call and have a pair of boots or shoes when he wanted them. The young man called several times, but would not tell his name nor residence, and it was near a year afterwards that it was discovered. Before that sum was worked out, he sent another ten guineas, and another equal sum before that was worked out. Some time afterwards he sent twenty guineas, and so on, always taking care to send a sum of money before the last was worked out. Himself, and his sons, two fine young gentlemen, continued to employ him as long as he remained in business; but to this day he will not allow his name to be mentioned, as it ought to be, a FRIEND. To another particular friend, in Lombard Street, he is much indebted, whom, as well as several others, we wish we were at liberty to name.

One thing, however, though it did not exactly balance the benefits accruing from the patronage of his real friends, was much against him at this period. A number of persons who *called* themselves his friends, and professed great zeal in the cause of Parliamentary Reform, employed, but have omitted to pay him to this day. Others borrowed money, and proved equally forgetful. The sums lost by this class of *pretended* friends, amounted, in the first year, to upwards of three hundred pounds, and has since encreased to a much greater sum. He was blamed for giving credit to such persons; but it is not easy to distinguish between the sincere and the designing: experience alone will teach this. Besides, he was himself naturally sincere and unsuspicious, which exposed him, more than men of a different character, to these sorts of depredations; and if such qualities are at all censurable, it must be confessed that there is a good deal of censure due to him.

Next to his pretended friends, may be ranged those who were covertly, and those who openly professed themselves his enemies; for though the tide of public opinion ran strongly in his favour, it could not be expected that the tools of his persecutors would refrain altogether from abuse. Accordingly he was attacked, by the hireling Ministerial press, in newspapers, and anonymous pamphlets; and although one would hardly think it possible, who did not know the constitution of that House in Mr. Pitt's days, there were Members of Parliament found possessed of so little decency and common sense, as, in in their places in the House of Commons, to apply the most unjustifiable epithets to him, and the other prisoners who had been honourably acquitted. The newspapers did not stick at any falsehood. The following extract is a fair, or rather foul, specimen of the methods which they pursued, to injure the character of a man, who, certainly, never did any thing to deserve such treatment at their hands.

"TO THE EDITOR OF THE COURIER.

"Sir

"On Wednesday, the 25th of October, the following Letter, and Statement, by '*An Old Inhabitant of Fleet Street*,' appeared in the '*True Briton*.' Knowing the greater part of the statement to be absolutely false, and having good reason to suppose it a malicious attempt to injure me in the opinion of the public, I thought it a duty which I owed to my friends, as well as to myself, to expose its falsehood and its malice; and accordingly desired the Editor of that Paper to insert the following Letter, which, however, he refused to do. I have, therefore, to request *you*, as a REAL friend to Truth, to assist me in rescuing my character from the attack of a milignant and cowardly Assassin, by giving a place in '*The Courier*,' to the following Letter, from,

"Sir,

"Your constant Reader,

"THOMAS HARDY."

"TO THE EDITOR OF THE TRUE BRITON.

"Sir,

"Not being in the habit of reading your Paper, I did not see the following Letter, and pretended Statement, which appeared in it on Wednesday last, till two or three days afterterwards, when it was shewn to me by a friend.—I do not wish to obtrude myself unnecessarily on the notice of the public; but I feel it a duty which, as a member of Society, I owe to myself, to repel an ill-founded, and apparently malicious and cowardly attack upon my character, in as public a manner as it has been made. I claim, therefore, from you, as a matter of right, that you will re-insert in your Paper the Letter and the Statement, together with the answer and observations which I have subjoined. I claim this as a right, which you cannot refuse me, consistently with your duty, as the Conductor of a Public Print, more especially of a Print, which, by its title, assumes to itself the peculiar character of ' *True*.'

" RIOT IN FLEET STREET.

" TO THE EDITOR OF THE TRUE BRITON.

" SIR,

" THE Riot at *Citizen* HARDY's house, in Fleet Street, having been the subject of much conversation, and but imperfectly represented in the Public Prints, I send you the following Statement, which I, as an Eye-Witness to the whole proceeding, can assure you is authentic.

" I am, Sir, your constant Reader,

" And very humble Servant,

" AN OLD INHABITANT OF FLEET STREET."

October 20, 1797.

" On Friday evening, the 13th instant, when the first account arrived of the glorious and truly important victory, gained by the gallant Admiral Duncan over the Dutch Fleet, a number of people paraded the streets, calling for 'Lights,' &c. A party of them being assembled at Drury Lane Theatre, for the same purpose, three or four *ill-looking fellows* began to harangue them on the impropriety of rejoicing at an event, which, they said, " would only tend to prolong the War;" and one of those *Seditious Emissaries* struck a lad a violent blow on the head with a bludgeon, merely for saying ' DUNCAN for ever!—No Jacobins!'— The Mob then surrounded them; and on examination they proved to be *Citizens* ASHLEY, HARDY, and others, Members of the *London Corresponding Society*. The people then expressed their indignation at these *spiteful Pseudo Reformers*, in a violent manner, and saluted them with hisses and groans, which were but a prelude to a shower of stones, mud, &c. which obliged the *Gentlemen* to decamp towards Prince's Street, with great precipitation, amidst the execrations of the spectators. Being *rather quick* in their flight, they escaped; and, *like men of courage, when out of danger*, they *valiantly* knocked down an aged and decrepid mendicant, and two or three boys, who were amusing themselves by letting off fireworks, and, like *victorious heroes*, they triumphantly marched off.

" The account of this *gallant action* was immediately carried to the Mob, who vowed revenge; but on Saturday night the *victorious Citizens* rested in peace. On Monday night, *Citizen* HARDY's house was filled with a set of Ruffians, armed with cutlasses, sword-sticks, bludgeons, &c. calling themselves Constables! Every house in Fleet Street was illuminated, except *Citizen* HARDY'S; of course a number of people collected opposite his house, and called for ' Lights!' The Ruffians inside immediately sallied out, and indiscriminately assaulted every person who had not the good fortune to escape. After the first shock, however, the Mob rallied, and growing formidable, by increase of numbers, they repelled the *Corresponding Army*, and broke most of *Citizen* HARDY's windows, amidst the cries of ' DUNCAN for ever! HARDY for ever! No Jacobins! No Lights, &c. &c. &c.'

" *Citizen* HARDY, finding his reforming sham Constables of no service, sent for the Military, and the Mob dispersed. This is a true statement of the affair: and it is hoped the Magistrates will prevent the *Corresponding Constables* from *breeding another riot*, as they were the sole cause of that above related."

"It may be true, for ought I know to the contrary, that the Riot at my house has been *imperfectly* represented in the public Prints; but I can take upon myself to say, that no other representation of it has been so replete with falsehood as that which is given in the above statement by 'An Old Inhabitant of Fleet Street,' which he, as an eye-witness to the whole proceeding, *says* he can assure you is authentic.

"Of my *own* positive knowledge, this statement is so far from being authentic, and such as an eye-witness who had any regard to truth would have given, that the greatest part of what relates to *me* is absolutely false; and, judging as a plain man of mere common sense, I believe that by far the greater part of the *whole* is a malicious fiction.

"It *may* be true, that a party of those who paraded the streets on Friday evening, the 13th instant, calling for 'Lights,' may have assembled at Drury Lane Theatre for that purpose; and it may possibly be true, though I do not believe it, because it is not probable that three or four such persons as this eye-witness calls *ill-looking fellows,* and *seditious emissaries,* may have begun to harangue the *mob,* on the impropriety of rejoicing at an event which, they said, 'would only tend to prolong the war:' but I am sure it cannot be true, that 'one of them struck a lad a violent blow on the head with a bludgeon,' merely for saying 'DUNCAN for ever! No Jacobins.' The men whom this 'Old Inhabitant' stigmatizes with the name of *seditious emissaries,* are not accustomed to carry *bludgeons,* or to use the arguments of *blows:* they leave such practices, and such conduct, to the *mob,* of which, if I may judge from the spirit of his statement, this eye-witness, probably, makes now and then a distinguished member. For the same reasons, I am sure it cannot be true, that these three or four *ill-looking fellows* afterwards 'knocked down an aged and decrepid mendicant, and two or three boys who were amusing themselves by letting off fireworks.'—The whole of this story carries in itself its own refutation. The ill-looking fellows are described to be only *three* or *four*: had their number been so small, it needed not to have been put in the alternative; an eye-witness to the whole proceedings might have stated precisely the exact number; but taking them to be *four*, it is not likely that one of so small a number, even of such *valiant* heroes, would have ventured to strike a lad a blow on the head with a bludgeon, in the presence of a *mob*, who are described to have been so numerous as to *surround* them; nor is it likely that when thus *surrounded*, and discovered to be *Citizens* ASHLEY, HARDY, &c. they would have been *permitted* to *escape* without some personal marks of mobish vengeance for the violent blow in the head with a bludgeon. The ' Old Inhabitant of Fleet Street,' indeed, states, that the hisses and groans with which they were at first saluted, were but a prelude to a shower of stones, mud, &c. which obliged the *gentlemen* to decamp with great precipitation; but how does he reconcile this to what he had just before related, that the mob *surrounded* them, and that, on *examination*, they were discovered to be *Citizens* ASHLEY, HARDY, &c.? If they were *surrounded*, and *examined*, there was hardly occasion for a shower of *stones, mud,* &c. which rather implies that the *ill-looking fellows* were at a *distance* from the mob: had they been *surrounded*, and *examined*, it is more probable they would have been *bludgeoned* than *stoned:* but, supposing them to have been *surrounded*, it must have required something more than *mere quickness* of *flight* to enable them to escape; they must have used something more *valiant* than swiftness of foot to break the *ring* with which they were *surrounded:* but the eye-witness says nothing of that kind. Suppose, however, they escaped, and knocked down the mendicant and the boys, how was the account of this *gallant action* immediately conveyed to the mob? Did the eye-witness, endowed with *quickness* of *pursuit*, equal to the *ill-looking fellows'* quickness of *flight*, convey the hasty intelligence? But the ' intelligence' was immediately conveyed to the mob, and the mob vowed revenge.' Had this been the case, it is probable that the *victorious Citizens*, instead of resting in peace on *Saturday* night, and enjoying their *triumph* till Monday, would, on *Friday* night, have suffered the threatened *revenge*.—So much for the *probability* of this ' authentic' account.

" The fact, so far as I am myself concerned, is this :—I do not *know* that there were either illuminations, or mob, on the evening of Friday the 13th, but by information which I have received since; and I was not, the whole of that evening, beyond the threshold of my own door; and, notwithstanding the confident assertion of the ' eye-witness to the whole proceeding,' who would have you suppose he is so well acquainted with my *person*, I was not one of the *three* or *four ill-looking fellows* surrounded, and *examined* by the mob at Drury Lane Theatre: and I am sure that the ' Old Inhabitant of Fleet Street,' if his countenance bears any relationship either to the wickedness of his heart, or to the weakness of his head, would, on examination, be found the *worse-looking fellow* of the two.

" Of the next paragraph, which pretends to state the transaction of Monday night, every syllable which relates to *me* is false, excepting the few words of it which state that most of my windows were broken. During the whole of Monday, the 15th instant, there certainly was not one *ruffian* in my house, unless the ' Old Inhabitant of Fleet Street' may have been there. I do not know, but from subsequent information, that every house in Fleet Street, but my own, was illuminated; but I know, that that exception gave no right to a lawless mob to break my windows to pieces. The fact is, that a mob, whether *composed* of such persons as the ' Old Inhabitant of Fleet Street,' or *instigated* by such persons, did on that evening begin to collect about my door, and to express a disposition to riot: about eight o'clock, therefore, an hour before my usual time, I had my shop shut up, to prevent the windows of it being broken through. There was not at any time, nor till a considerable time after, any person in my house but myself and my ordinary inmates. I had formed no positive determination as to illuminating or not, till a little before nine o'clock, when hearing a violent knocking at the street door, I went down stairs and opened it; a considerable number of people were there; I asked what they wanted; a baker's man asked me if I did not intend to illuminate; I told him he had no right to ask me that question, and desired him to go about his business: a voice from the crowd cried out, 'That's right, HARDY; don't illuminate;' on which I shut the door. It *might* have been **prudent** for me, in the *first instance*, to illuminate; but I did not like the idea of compulsion: I do not relish the government of a mob, though I cannot say I rejoice much in the success of a war which its abettors pretend to have been undertaken for the purpose of suppressing anarchy and confusion.—From the mixed cries of 'DUNCAN for ever,' and 'HARDY for ever,' I supposed the crowd was composed of different sets of people; and I have since been told, and I believe it to be true, that a number of my friends, apprehensive that my person and property were in danger, assembled from different quarters, with a determination, at the risk of their lives, to defend both; and I have understood that they did so most manfully; but there was no person in my house, ruffian, or otherwise, armed with cutlass, sword-stick, or bludgeon, or that assumed the character of constable. It is true that after the affair was over, some of my friends were received into the house, and partook of such sober refreshment as it afforded; and this circumstance, perhaps, the eye-witness, if indeed he had *any fact* in contemplation, has converted into an assertion, that on Monday night my house was filled with a set of ruffians, armed with cutlasses, swordsticks, bludgeons, &c. calling themselves constables! To my friends, on that occasion, I am assuredly much indebted. A few *such* trusty friends, on a similar occasion, on the 11th of June, 1794, might probably have prevented the fatal effect which afterwards ensued: the candles which were then placed in my windows proved NO PROTECTION to the HELPLESS and the INNOCENT! and I have had too much experience of the wicked and persecuting spirit of such men as the 'Old Inhabitant of Fleet Street,' not to be satisfied that a few candles placed in my windows, would have proved at least as feeble a protection on the *late* occasion as they did on the *former*.

"'*Citizen* HARDY,' says the 'Old Inhabitant of Fleet Street,' 'finding his sham constables of no service, sent for the military, and the *mob* dispersed.'—It is true, that when the conduct of the misguided populace gave me every reason to suppose that nothing short of making one grand illumination of my house was their diabolical object, I did, less from personal consideration than to render easy the minds of my neighbours, send for a party of the London Militia, who did not, however, arrive till after the contest was decided in favour of my friends. Notwithstanding this, I think it an act of justice due to the Gentleman to whom the application was made, to state his conduct on that occasion:—Sir WATKIN LEWES, to whom my friend carried my message, had a Military Officer with him. When my friend explained his business, this Officer said, ' I suppose Mr. HARDY has put no lights in his windows; go home and tell him to put lights in his windows, and the mob will disperse.' Sir WATKIN LEWES prevented my friend's reply by saying, ' Sir, we have nothing to do with a man's political principles; our duty is to protect every Citizen of London who requires our protection; tell Mr. HARDY that I shall send the Guard immediately.'

"The 'Old Inhabitant' concludes with a hope, that 'the *Magistrates* will prevent the *Corresponding Constables* from *breeding* another riot, as *they* were the sole cause of the above related.' I am not disposed to quibble on the structure of a sentence, or I might accuse the 'Old Inhabitant' of asserting that the *Magistrates* were the sole cause of the riot. I impute no fault to the Magistrates; had they suspected an intention to produce one, they probably would have prevented it; and I hope, that if, unfortunately, any peaceable inhabitant of this City shall hereafter be so shamefully attacked as I have been, the Magistrates will shew that the Police of the City does not permit such outrages to pass with impunity. There is no doubt but the ' Old Inhabitant means to assert, that those whom he calls the *Corresponding Constables* were the cause of the riot. The assertion is absolutely false, and *maliciously* false: the riot was most unquestionably *bred* by such men as the ' Old Inhabitant,' who seem to know no better mode of supporting *order* and *regular* Government than by encouraging the disorders of an unruly mob!"

"THOMAS HARDY,

October 30, 1797. " *No.* 161, *Fleet Street.*"

But his traducers did not confine their abuse to pamphlets and papers; they gave vent to it on all possible occasions. A single instance of this kind, as it is rather a laughable one, may be mentioned. In the Summer of 1795, when his business became so slack as to admit of his absence for a short time, he took a journey to Leicester, at the invitation of several friends then personally unknown to him, but from whom he had received considerable orders before. At Northampton, one gentleman, who had travelled in the coach from London, left, and another took his place. This latter gentleman happened to take up one of Hardy's shop cards, which a lady had laid down on the parlour table where the passengers breakfasted. As soon as he perceived what it was, he threw it down again with the greatest indignation, accompanying the action with some indecent and opprobrious expressions not fit to be repeated; and added, that the jury which had acquitted him consisted of a set of villains, &c. One of the ladies present, observed, that he subjected himself to severe punishment, by animadverting, in such unbecoming terms, on the decision of an English jury. This reproof silenced him, and he spoke very little more during the journey. When he did speak a few words, it was in such a cross and ill-natured manner that he became a subject of amusement to the passengers. The rest of the company were very cheerful, and the silent gentleman's remarks, and the ready and well-merited reproof which these remarks had received, introduced the trials as the subject of conversation, in which Hardy, who was personally unknown to any of the company, joined.

When the passengers were parting at the Bell Inn, Leicester, he stepped up to the crabbed gentleman, took him by the hand, and said to him, "Friend, be so good as to tell your acquaintance, that you have had the mortification to travel in the same coach with that Hardy whom you have been so illiberally abusing. I am that Hardy— farewell!" He stood with astonishment, and went away without saying a word, to all appearance, really mortified; to the great amusement of the other passengers.

Mr. Phillips, now Sir Richard, the bookseller, then resident in Leicester, was the first who called upon, and introduced him to many other kind friends. The next day he set out for Nottingham, with his good friend, Thomas Simpson, to whom he was introduced by Mr. Phillips. At Nottingham he remained a week, and was kindly and hospitably treated by some of the principal people of the town, from whom he received considerable orders.

From Nottingham he crossed the country to Derby, where he stayed two or three days with some friends, and then returned to London, highly pleased with his journey.

The next Summer he took a journey to Suffolk, and stayed a few days at Bury St. Edmunds, where he was kindly received by Mr. Buck, Mr. Vardy, and several other friends. From Bury he went to Norwich, where he met with some friends whom he knew, and by whom he was introduced to many others, some of them the principal people of the town, who treated him with particular kindness and attention. He next went to Yarmouth, and returned to London by Woodbridge, and Ipswich, at each of which places he met with such civilities and kindness as he never can forget.

Finding that he could not, with any hopes of advantage, continue in such an unfrequented situation as that in which he had recommenced business, he removed into Fleet Street, in September, 1797. There he became a Freeman of the Cordwainers Company, and Liveryman of the Needlemakers Company, and carried on his business with some success until 1815, when he retired; in what circumstances will appear sufficiently plain from the following correspondence.

"Dear Sir,

"I shall never forget the kindly manner in which you expressed your wish to serve me, when I had the pleasure of meeting you in the Committee Room, during the last election; and it was to me quite unexpected. I am sensible that you will excuse me for troubling you with the following facts, which concern myself, and which I shall state as briefly as possible. A few years before I left Fleet Street, I found my business gradually declining, owing to several causes. The general failure of trade, and bankruptcy of tradesmen about that time, the great cause of which, many worthy men, and their families knew, and felt to their sorrowful experience. Of the consequences of that general calamity I had my share, for almost every month I suffered a loss, less or more, by bankrupts, or by some compounding with their creditors, and by others exiling themselves. I had also outlived so many of my friends, who were in the habit of employing me, but who had passed that bourne from whence no traveller returns; and, likewise, my getting old, and old fashioned, so that I could not keep up with the rapid changes of fashion which the young require, and are fond of, and which it is quite necessary for tradesmen to attend to, however trifling they may be. In the last year or two, my difficulties rapidly increased, and I also found my health much impaired, from anxiety, losses, and crosses, which at last decided me to wind up my business, and dispose of it in the best way I could, while I had some little property remaining. I made no one acquainted with my circumstances, and I believe no one suspected that I was going behind; for with those with whom I had any dealings, my payments were regular, although, towards the close, I had great difficulty to keep my credit good. It was always a happy thing for me that my wants were few, and they are still diminishing, and my family small, only my dear Sister and myself. After collecting all debts due to me that I could possibly get, which amounted to but a small sum, compared to the debts now totally lost, some from real inability to pay, and others from causes not so excusable : when I had disposed of all belonging to the business, with the lease of the house, and settled all claims on me, *I retired*, at Midsummer, 1815, with a clear £700. The next consideration was, how this sum was to be disposed of to the best advantage for our future subsistence. It was too small a sum with which to purchase an annuity for myself and Sister. I therefore calculated, that from the then state of my health, that my life was apparently fast drawing to a close, and that by confining my expenses, so as not to exceed £100. a year, as having no other income, it would be more, perhaps, than sufficient, without being troublesome to my friends, for I was very unwilling to let my situation or circumstances be known. But when I was relieved from the cares, perplexities, and precariousness of a losing concern, my mind became easy and contented, and I soon recovered my health. And now, upwards of seven years and a half afterwards, there is but a little of the £700. remaining; but, perhaps, it may be enough, for if I see the third of next month, March, I shall then enter on my 72d year. And when I take a review of past occurrences, I find that I have abundant cause to be grateful.

" Be so good, dear Sir, to accept of my sincere wish, that you may long live in health and happiness, to enjoy the beneficial effects, which I hope are beginning to appear, of your long and honest efforts, with others, to benefit your country.

" THOMAS HARDY,
" 30, *Queen's Row, Pimlico.*"

4th February, 1823.
To Sir Francis Burdett, Bart.

" DEAR HARDY,

" I SHALL have great pleasure in rendering you assistance, having great regard for you, as an honest, sensible, ill-treated man. I wish you to be more explicit as to your desires, and, in the mean time, beg of you to accept the enclosed*

" With great regard,

St. James's Place,   " F. BURDETT."
February 8th, 1823.

" *St. James's Place, May 9th,* 1823.

" DEAR HARDY,

" I TOLD you long ago to set your mind at rest, and have written a line to Mr. Friend, in answer to one he sent me concerning you. I propose to him to get an annuity for you of £100. a year, which I take to be about as much as would make you and your Sister comfortable; I will advance one half, and five other persons who know and respect your understanding and integrity, will advance £10. a piece. The money will be placed in Mr. Friend's hands, and you will be pleased to draw it out just as you have occasion for it.

" I am laid up with the gout, which makes writing painful,

---

* £10.

but would not lose a moment in setting your mind at ease. I hope your Sister is well.

"Yours, very sincerely,

"F. BURDETT."

"DEAR SIR,

"I do assure you it is with grateful satisfaction I have to acknowledge your liberality to me, as mentioned in your letter on Friday last. From the moment you told me to make my mind easy respecting my future subsistence, and knowing so well your disposition to do good, I was sure that you would fulfil your benevolent intentions, therefore I hope you will excuse me when I state that my writing to Mr. Friend, afterwards, did not arise from any doubt on that head, but because I thought that the burden of my support ought not to rest on one friend only, however able and willing that friend may be. A few minutes after I received yours on Friday, I had a note, by the twopenny post, from Mr. Friend, desiring me to call on him. I have not yet seen him, for I have not been out for this week past; but as the weather is getting more favourable for invalids, I hope to be able to call on him in a few days. Will you be so good as to offer to those five Gentlemen whom you mentioned, my sincere thanks for their kindness to me. I hope you are now fast recovering, and have dislodged that troublesome and cruel enemy the gout. Be so good, dear Sir, as to accept my sincere good wishes for a speedy restoration of your health.

14*th May*, 1823. "THOMAS HARDY."
To Sir Francis Burdett, Bart.

"DEAR SIR,

"I CANNOT help troubling you with a few lines at this time, which I hope you will excuse. God knows whether I may have another opportunity to offer my grateful acknowledgement for your annual kindness to me, for these five years now closed. I have now, on the 3rd of last March, entered on the 77th year of my journey of life, for which I have great reason to be grateful to a gracious God, who has preserved and protected me during so long a period, and blessed me with so many kind friends, and in some perilous circumstances too. Even this 29th of May, 1794, is memorable as the anniversary of my being sent to the *Tower;* some of my valued friends who are no more, having been sent before me to that *Fortress,* all on a charge of High Treason, by a Privy Council of erring men; so that I am now thirty-four years older than they intended that I should be.

" I beg now to state, for your information, the amount of the different sums which I have drawn for yearly, from my kind friend *Mr. Friend,* who was good enough to take the troublesome office of Treasurer, but has now transferred it to my friend, *Mr. Place,* for what reason I do not know. I fear that it may be I had drawn too much from the account, or for some other impropriety on my part; if it be so, I am very sorry for it. My frequent applications to him were always readily answered, without a hint of that sort.

" Received from Mr. Friend, at several times, from the 1st of May, 1823, to May, 1824			....	£100 0 0
" Ditto,	Ditto,	1st of May, 1824, to May, 1825		100 0 0
" Ditto,	Ditto,	May, 1825, to May, 1826		130 0 0
" Ditto,	Ditto,	May, 1826, to May, 1827		120 0 0
" Ditto,	from Mr. Place, altered to the 1st of June, 1827, to June, 1828 ..			109 12 0

" I have now, Dear Sir, to beg that you will be so good to accept my sincere best wishes that you may long enjoy excellent health, and that you may be able to advocate, with success, the great cause of Civil Liberty, and the happiness of your country and your fellow men, as you have hitherto done.

29th May, 1828.   " THOMAS HARDY."
To Sir Francis Burdett, Bart.

"DEAR SIR,

"I HOPE you are quite well. I congratulate you on the pleasing prospect before us, which I hope we shall before long fully enjoy, that great national blessing—a *Parliamentary Reform*, which your great talents, years ago, were often exerted to obtain. Although not then successful, yet your efforts were not lost, for you then sowed abundance of good seed, which has been springing up ever since, and which I hope will now produce a plentiful harvest for the benefit of your fellow countrymen. I am much pleased with the present Government; I believe they are sincere, and will be active in their exertions to promote that great object to its completion. I am pleased to see so many converts to the important cause of Parliamentary Reform; some from conviction of its justice, and others from necessity. I hope the Ministers will be well supported by all the *old* and *true* Reformers. Perhaps, you may smile when I tell you, that I am now, *for the first time*, in my humble measure, a supporter of Ministers. I greatly rejoice to see the great cause of Civil Liberty prospering, not only in this country, but all over Europe, and that I have lived so many years to witness it, having entered on the 80th year of my journey of life, the 3rd of this month of March. I hope you will excuse me for troubling you with this, and accept my best wishes that you may enjoy long life in health and happiness.

"THOMAS HARDY,
"*30, Queen's Row, Pimlico.*"

7th March, 1831.
Sir Francis Burdett, Bart. M.P.

To this correspondence with the most upright, most intrepid, and most persevering Statesman of our own country, may appositely succeed the following Letter from Hardy to Lafayette, with that great and eminently virtuous man's answer.

" DEAR AND RESPECTED SIR,

"ALTHOUGH I have not had the happiness to see you, yet you are no stranger to me, for I have followed you in all your pereginations with my good wishes, high approbation, and esteem, for your unwearied exertions to promote the happiness of your fellow men. Ever since the beginning of the American Revolution, I remember well your laudable efforts, together with that extraordinary man Washington, to gain that great object for which the brave Americans were contending—their emancipation from a foreign yoke, which they at last effected; and now they are a great and prosperous nation. I have great pleasure to remark, that you and I have been fellow labourers in the great cause of Civil Liberty, ever since that important period. We may now be permitted to rejoice together with the great body of the friends of liberty, that their honest efforts have not been lost. It was a maxim of the celebrated Reformer, Dr. John Jebb, that *no effort is lost*. Permit me now to congratulate you on the late glorious Revolution in France, in July last; it has no parallel in ancient or modern history. I also well remember the first Revolution in France, about forty years ago; and I am very happy when I recollect that I was instrumental in sending the *first* Congratulatory Address from this country, from *The London Corresponding Society*, to the *National Convention of France*, with which they appeared to be so well pleased, that it was read in the Convention, ordered to be printed, sent to the eighty-four Departments, and to be read at the head of the Armies of France. When the Paris newspapers, having that Address, came to London, it astonished and highly pleased the people; but not so the Government. When that useful and important Society, the fruit of whose labours the British nation are reaping at this day, unanimously voted that Address, they deputed four trusty friends to convey it in the safest and quickest way possible. Being the *Secretary*, and in fact the *founder* of the Society, I waited on *Monsieur Chaveline, privately*, to know whether he would convey it. He readily consented, and ordered the deputation to wait on him the next day, at 11 o'clock: they, of course, punctually attended, and read the Address to him, with which he was much pleased, and promised to send it speedily. The Address was signed the 27th of September, 1792, *Maurice Margarot*, Chairman, *Thomas Hardy*, Secretary. That period is worth referring to, were I in Paris, if any of the records of the Convention are now in existence.

"I cannot help mentioning to you how much I am pleased with the Revolution which has taken place in this country, for *revolution* it is. *The King, and his Ministers, are now turned Parliamentary Reformers!* They are guilty of the very same crime, if crime it be, with which Parliamentary Reformers, in the year 1794, were charged by the infamous Government of *Pitt, Dundas,* and *Grenville*, the greatest crime known in our laws—*High Treason.* Many were imprisoned, some were banished, and three were tried for it; but an English Jury had a very different opinion of the criminality of their conduct, and honourably *acquitted* them. I rejoice that it has pleased God to spare my life so long, being now in my 80th year, to witness this grand and beneficial change which has taken place in this country; and also great changes all over Europe. I ardently wish the oppressed people of every country may be relieved from their oppressors.

"Political knowledge is making a great and rapid progress; it is now diffused among all classes. The press—the printing press is performing wonders. It was a maxim of the great *Lord Bacon,* that *knowledge is power.* I fear that I have encroached upon your valuable time with my garrulity, if you will condescend to take time to read this long letter. I shall now conclude with my sincere best wishes, that you may enjoy long life, in health and happiness.

11th April, 1831.   "THOMAS HARDY,
Lafayette, France.   "30, *Queen's Row, Pimlico.*"

"My friend, Mr. Lewis, has been kind enough to say that he will convey this to you."

"*La Grange, July 3d,* 1831.

"My Dear Sir,

"Your much valued favour, April 11, has but this day been delivered to me. The wishes of the London Corresponding Society, for universal freedom, have been expressed in the beginning of the French Revolution; and now we can congratulate each other on the electric stroke of the French week of last July, and upon the happy spirit of Parliamentary Reform which is now prevailing in England. This mutual fellow-feeling must take place of the prejudices which aristocracy and despotism have so long kept up between nations. Be pleased to accept my acknowledgements for the sentiments you were so kind to express in my behalf, as well as the assurance of my good wishes and sincere regard.

"LAFAYETTE."

Thomas Hardy, Esq.

Up to the present day, his kind and benevolent friend—the friend of his country—the friend of mankind—with the other gentlemen alluded to in the above letters, have continued liberally to support him. He has ever strongly relied on Providence, and has not been deceived nor disappointed. He has now passed the middle of the 81st year of his age, and can look back on many of the actions of his life with approbation. Like all human creatures, he has, in many things, failed, and come short; but he commits himself with confident hope to the mercy of his Creator and his Redeemer, and awaits the period of his release from this state of mortality with patience and resignation.

APPENDIX.

LETTER TO A FRIEND,

WRITTEN IN 1799.

" DEAR SIR,

" You have frequently expressed a wish to know something of the history of the *London Corresponding Society*, but not being qualified to write a regular history of it, perhaps I cannot do better than narrate to you, occasionally by letter, what information comes within my own knowledge, respecting that important and interesting Society, which appeared to have alarmed the Government, and greatly to have agitated the nation. Much opposition to it was excited, and much calumny, abuse, and persecution the Members experienced, both as a body, and as individuals. I shall endeavour to give you a true, and as concise an account as possible, of the rise and progress of it, together with its motives and design.

Being the founder of *The London Corresponding Society*, *(which I now avow,)* it may reasonably be expected that I should give an accurate account of its formation and progress, up to a certain period, having been indefatigable in promoting the great object which the Society had in view, *a Reform in the representation of the people in the Commons House of Parliament*, which I was only the feeble instrument of reviving. The public and private correspondence which I had with different classes on that subject, both before it was instituted, and afterwards, was extensive, comparatively speaking. If endeavouring to form an association, thereby to effect a reformation in Parliament, and in full hope, through that medium, to obtain a redress of the many grievances which the people have thousands of times ineffectually complained of—If an attempt of this sort was either treason, or sedition; I certainly was very culpable; probably our rulers thought so; for they had many secret agents, or, in other words, spies and informers, employed to report to them what was going on, and the Society was very open in all its measures; indeed, their object was publicity, the more public the better. Had the agents reported to their employers, fairly and honestly, what the conduct of the Society was, they could not have been blamed; but it seems that would not have answered their purpose, for it evidently appeared afterwards, that they fully designed to effect its ruin at its commencement, and to destroy thousands afterwards, of the best, yea, even the most *loyal* men in the nation; men who were sincere friends to peace, and the welfare of mankind; not sinecurists, nor idle drones in society, but active and useful citizens. Part of my correspondence, both with Societies and individuals, was made public on the late *State Trials*, as they are termed, as much as suited the purpose of our prosecutors; but a great part was withheld by the Ministers, or some other persons for them. I do not wish to charge the Ministers with more injustice than they deserve, for God knows they had enough of their own to answer for. That which was kept back, might have been of much use in my defence, had it been needful; but as the trial terminated in a verdict of acquittal, there was quite enough, from their own showing, to prove that their charge against us was iniquitous.

"Some letters and papers, which escaped the search of the *legal* plunderers, on the 12th of May, 1794, (the day on which I was apprehended by a warrant of the Secretary of State, on a charge of High Treason, signed Henry Dundas,) I meant to give my friends and the public, that they might, if they pleased, re-judge me; but the interest for such is now gone by. Much political information I frequently received from Gentlemen experienced in the cause of Reform, which was communicated to the Society, and received with great approbation, and which was of much use in regulating their conduct as a young Society. Inexperienced people are liable to be led into error, and injudicious conduct, by designing men. Attempts of that sort were sometimes frustrated in good time. It has been often said by some, who were afterwards discovered not to be friendly to Reform, that Democrats, or Reformers, ought not to have any secrets; insinuating as if the Society had something more in view than what they avowed. It was also often asked, and they appeared very anxious to know, who was the *founder* of the Society; as if, by ascertaining that fact, they would discover an important secret. The question was always evaded, because of the obscurity and unimportance in Society of the founder, and that it might be better esteemed by the public, and more respectable, agreeably to the received idea of respectability, and that they might attend more particularly to the object which the thing formed had in view, than to who was the framer of it. But it was established on too virtuous a principle to be suffered long to retain its good name among that class, whose chief interest, on that subject, was to deceive and calumniate. The rotten Borough holders, who are enemies to Reform, were all up in arms against the Society: for if a full, fair, and free representation of the people in Parliament succeeded, their corrupt gain was gone, and the people's rights obtained. I flattered myself that if a Society were formed on the principles of the representative system, men of talents, who had time to devote for promoting the cause, would step forward, and we, who were the framers of it, who had neither time to spare from our daily employments, nor talents for conducting so important an undertaking, would draw into the back ground. I was also encouraged to hope, from the then favourable state of things, and from the vast number of friends to Reform, who had assisted for that purpose, in the years 1780-81-82, ten years before, in every county in the nation, of men of the first rate abilities and consequence in the country, who, I supposed, were not all dead, and who had not altogether relinquished the idea of prosecuting the subject of a Parliamentary Reform, but waited only for a favourable opportunity to come forward again to testify their firm regard to the cause of human happiness. But it was soon found that an alarm was created among that class, by the uncommon appearance of the popular Societies, and their active exertions in diffusing political knowledge among their brethren. Many in the Society might have been found more fit for the station which I held in it, but none could be more sincerely desirous of success, nor more zealous and active in promoting the object which the Society had in view, viz. *a thorough, or Radical Reformation in Parliament.* That great object once gained, then there was a point fixed to which all our complaints of injuries and oppression might be directed for redress—AN HONEST PARLIAMENT. The subject of Reform is nearly as old as corruption itself; for ever since rulers have exercised their usurped power over the people, there has been found some men who are more alive to the sufferings of their fellow men than the bulk of their brethren are, who have called out loudly for Reform: and it has often happened that some of the meanest of the people have been the instruments of effecting much good. Great events have often been the consequence of apparently insignificant beginnings; for there have been instruments raised up, from among the meanest of mankind, to produce the greatest changes that have taken place in the world. Many examples might be given; but it appears needless; they are so well known, almost to every one who is only partially acquainted with history. How to eradicate gross abuses, and renovate the original compact between the governors and the people, have been the constant study, and unwearied labour of good men in all ages. Wishing to copy from our forefathers, we may expect the same wages, slander, and persecution. The oppressions of our fellow men are numerous, caused by ————. This would lead into a variety of subjects very unpleasant to contemplate, or to describe. The causes are obvious. The poor, and middling classes of the people, are, to their woeful experience, but too well acquainted with them. In the months of November, and December, 1791, my leisure hours were employed in reading some political tracts, which I had formerly perused with much pleasure, during the American War: among which were a great variety published *gratis*, by the Society for Constitutional Information, at that time; and some excellent pamphlets, written by *Granville Sharp, Major Cartwright, Dr. Jebb, Dr. Price, Thomas Day, Rev. Mr. Stone, Capel Lofft, John Horne Tooke, John Trenchard, Thomas Gordon, Lord Somers, Duke of Richmond, Sir William Jones, Davenent*, &c. &c.

" From the small tracts and pamphlets, written by these *really* great men, much political information was diffused through the nation, at that period, by their benevolent exertions; the beneficial effects of which are felt to the present day. The sphere of life in which I was necessarily placed, allowed me no time to read long books; therefore, those smaller ones were preferred, being within the compass of my ability to purchase, and time to peruse, and, I believe, they are the most useful to any class of readers. Dr. Price's celebrated Treatise on Civil Liberty, was the first that confirmed me in the opinion, that the American War was both impolitic and unjust. The above-mentioned worthies laboured hard to correct the prevailing abuses of the Government, in their time, and their zealous efforts have not been in vain; for, by their sensible and spirited writings, level to common capacities, thousands of the people have been informed what are their rights, privileges, and duties, as men, and citizens; and how they have often been despoiled of their valuable rights, both by fraud and force. But do not despair, brave *living* patriots; persevere, enlighten the people, and the country will be saved from the bad government of rapacious men. Knowledge has made a rapid and a sure progress within these thirty years, therefore continue your efforts. Dr. Jebb's favourite maxim is, that NO EFFORT IS LOST.

> " Resist whatever in a State is base,
> " If Heaven has given you talents, by your pen;
> " Thus, without noise, you may prevent disgrace,
> " And save your country from injurious men."

" After reading, and attentively considering the short state of the representation, which was published by the Society for Constitutional Information, at that time; although it was an imperfect statement, yet it was very evident that a *Radical Reform in Parliament* was quite necessary; for it is as clear as a mathematical axiom that the people are unrepresented, or misrepresented. The result of all my consideration of the subject, was an attempt to form a Society of another class of the people, to effect that most desirable and necessary Reform, which had baffled the united associations of men of the greatest talents, worth, and consequence in the nation. In order to promote that desirable end, I drew up the outlines of a plan, with rules and regulations; plain and simple as they were, they served as a foundation on which to rear one of the most orderly, and important political societies that ever appeared in this country. The first meeting of this Society took place on the evening of the 25th of January, 1792, at the sign of the Bell, Exeter Street, Strand: eight persons signed the articles, in a book which I had previously prepared, and paid one penny each, agreeably to one of the articles: then I gave each a ticket, on which was written the name of the Society, with the No. 1, 2, 3, &c. and the Member's name written on the back. The next thing these eight persons considered, was to choose from among themselves some trusty servants, to conduct the business of that friendly and well meaning company. They appointed me Treasurer and Secretary. There they stumbled at the threshhold, in allowing *two very important offices to be filled by one person.* The amount of cash in the Treasurer's hand, the first Meeting, was, *eightpence*. Although we were, at first, but few in number, and humble in situation and circumstances, yet we wished to consider how to remedy the many defects and abuses which had crept into the administration of Government: and in prosecuting our enquiries, we soon discovered, that *gross ignorance, and prejudice*, in the bulk of the nation, was the greatest obstacle to the obtaining redress. Therefore, our honest aim was to have a well regulated, and orderly Society formed, for the purpose of dispelling that ignorance, and prejudice, as far as possible, and to instill into their minds, by means of the printing press, in a legal and constitutional way, a sense of their rights as freemen, and of their duty to themselves, and their posterity, as good citizens, and hereditary guardians of the liberties transmitted to them by their forefathers. On the Monday following, which was the first of February, there were eight more added to the number, and increased the funds of the Society to *two shillings*. The third Meeting, nine more were added, which encreased the number to twenty-five, and the sum in the treasury to *four shillings and one penny*. A mighty sum! They increased in knowledge, in numbers, and information, after that, every week: and on the 2d of April, 1792, the first Address and Resolutions of the Society were printed, in which their principles and design were clearly stated to the public, and published in the Newspapers; and from that time there was a rapid increase of new Members, and new Societies were starting up in various parts of the country, printing and publishing addresses and resolutions, declarative of their principles and designs. This little Society, consisting, at first, of not more than eight plain, homely, and obscure citizens, soon attained a magnitude beyond any thing of the kind ever attempted. Such is the prevalence of truth, and the force of her arguments, that before the end of the year, the London Corresponding Society had formed an intimate connection, and correspondence with every Society in Great Britain; all of whom were subsequently instituted, for the express purpose of obtaining, by all legal and constitutional means, a *Radical Reform in the Commons' House of Parliament.*

"Accept, Dear Sir, the best wishes of

"THOMAS HARDY."

"A copy of the above Letter I read to the company present on the 5th of November, 1824, at the Crown and Anchor Tavern, Strand, being thirty years, that day, after the event which they were then met to commemorate. "T. H."

"TRIAL BY JURY—REFORM.

"On Tuesday evening a body of respectable individuals met, as usual, at the Crown Tavern, on Clerkenwell Green, to celebrate the Acquittal of THOMAS HARDY and others, and the Trial by Jury. The veteran Reformist was not present; but the following interesting Letter was read from the Chair :*—

London, Nov. 5, 1816.

"DEAR SIR,

"I HAVE, for the last twenty-one years, had the pleasure of annually meeting our friends, who are to assemble to-day at the Crown Tavern, to commemorate the important event which took place on the 5th of November, 1794—an event important, indeed, to the fate of thousands, and in which it was my lot to be particularly concerned. As I am removed to a great distance from their house of meeting, I have to beg that they will excuse my personal attendance, assuring them that my kind wishes towards them, and my patriotic feelings towards my country, have undergone neither change nor diminution during the lapse of years. Situated as I am, I hope

* When this Letter was sent, I was afraid that I could not attend, but I did attend. T. H.

for their indulgence for my absence, and I shall hear with pleasure of the hilarity and public spirit with which, I trust, their Meeting will be inspired. My ardent wish is, that, as the first measure of salvation for our country, they will not forget to keep alive THE GREAT CAUSE OF PARLIAMENTARY REFORM—the claiming of which, by a great part of the nation in the year 1793, afforded the then Administration a pretext for involving the country in all the calamities of war; the object of which war was, to oppose a barrier to the progress of the intellect of mankind, but more immediately to divert the attention of the people of Britain from their domestic oppressions. Here I cannot omit bringing to your pleasing recollections, those much to be respected Members of Parliament who advocated the cause of the people, and stated, in forcible language, the necessity of a Reform in the Representation of the People in the House of Commons, and endeavoured, by every means in their power, to prevent the Government from interfering with the internal affairs of REPUBLICAN FRANCE. The fatal consequences such interference has brought upon our country, and upon all Europe, the people are, to their woeful experience, now severely feeling, and which was clearly foretold at that time by many of those friends to mankind; but they were, like all good men, treated as fools and enemies to their country, by their country's *real* enemies.

" Perhaps it may be desirable, for the information of those who have come into existence since the commencement of THE LONDON CORRESPONDING SOCIETY, to attempt to state concisely the rise, progress, and object of that Institution. This Society (which has been so basely calumniated) began in the latter end of 1791, in consequence of a conversation I had with a friend respecting the unequal Representation of the People in Parliament. That conversation suggested the propriety of instituting a Society, with the view of ascertaining the opinion of the people on that question, by corresponding with other Societies that might be formed, having the same object in view, as well as with public-spirited individuals. The idea was mentioned to another friend or two, by whom it was readily approved, and this was further communicated to others. At last a Society was formed, and afterwards increased to a magnitude which alarmed the Boroughmongers, and all who had an interest in perpetuating the system of deception and injustice, that was beginning to extend its baneful influence. I intend not in this Letter to give a regular history of this Society, although I have sufficient materials; it may, however, be presented to the public on some future occasion.

"The first Meeting of the London Corresponding Society was held on the 25th of January, 1792, consisting of eight persons; and after arranging the form, and terms of admitting Members, it was agreed, in order to pay the expense of stationery, printing, and postage of letters, that each Member should continue to pay weekly one penny. This plan was first carried into practice by this Society, with great effect. How strange, and how very amusing it was for me, to see a plan exactly similar recommended to the adoption of the British and Foreign School Society, by a Royal Duke, five and twenty years afterwards, a plan which is also now in full practice by Missionary and Bible Societies. The same means that were used to promote the success of Parliamentary Reform, in 1794, were charged as a crime (among many other wicked charges,) against the London Corresponding Society.

"Although we were but a small number of well-meaning, sober, and industrious men, yet we presumed to take into our considerations the many defects and abuses which had crept into the state of the Representation. Considering that the gross ignorance, and prejudice of the British nation, were the greatest obstacles to the obtaining redress, our efforts were directed to the formation of a well regulated and orderly Society, for the sole purpose of printing and distributing small political tracts on the subject, which it was enabled to do to a great extent, from the penny subscription. The Society was unceasing in its attempts to dispel that ignorance and prejudice, which has been so fatal to this country and to mankind, conveying to their minds a knowledge of their rights as freemen, and of their duty to themselves and their posterity, as good citizens, and hereditary guardians of the liberties transmitted to them by their forefathers. Happily, many of the young men, who were Members, have acknowledged, and do still acknowledge, their great obligations to that much defamed Society, for their well-regulated conduct in after life, and have given a practical refutation to the charges exhibited against them, in the continued respectability of their lives, in the morality of their conduct, during a lengthened period of years, and in the elevated and opulent situations to which some have since attained in society.

" The form of admitting Members was very simple; it was merely by proposing the three following questions; and if they were answered in the affirmative, then their names and address were entered in a book, and a ticket given to them, on which was written their own name, and that of the Society, with the motto, UNITE, PERSEVERE, *and be* FREE :—

" *Question First,*—Are you convinced that the Parliamentary Representation of this country is inadequate and imperfect ?

" *Second,*—Are you thoroughly persuaded that the welfare of these kingdoms require that every adult person, in possession of his reason, and not incapacitated by crimes, should have a vote for a Member of Parliament ?

" *Third,*—Will you endeavour, by all justifiable means, to promote such Reformation in Parliament ?"

" The second week of meeting there were eight more Members added to the Society, and the week following nine, which made the number 25; and the sum in the treasury amounted to four shillings and one penny.—The following questions were then submitted for discussion :—

" *First,*—Is there any necessity for a Reformation in the present state of the Representation in the British House of Commons ?

" *Second,*—Would there be any utility in a Parliamentary

Reform? or, in other words, is there just ground to believe that a Reformation in Parliament will be of essential good to the nation?

"*Third*,—Have we, who are Tradesmen, Shopkeepers, and Mechanics, any right to seek to obtain a Parliamentary Reform?"

"These questions were debated in the Society five nights successively, in every point of view in which we were capable of presenting the subject to our minds; and, after mature deliberation, they were all decided in the affirmative.

"The first Address and Resolutions which the Society printed, and which were published very extensively, were dated the 2d of April, 1792. From that time the Society became known to the public. Societies were then formed in different parts of England, Scotland, and Ireland, in quick succession, for the same laudable object. A constant correspondence was afterwards kept up with each of these Societies. The London Corresponding Society was considered the Parent Society. This was the reason why Burke, in one of his mad rants in the House of Commons, designated it as 'The Mother of all Mischief.'

"At this period the numbers increased rapidly; and political knowledge was diffused generally throughout the nation, by the means of small Tracts, which were well adapted for giving information to persons of every capacity, and also by political discussions and conversations in the various Meetings. The number of Members in the different Societies increased, in about two years, to an amount far exceeding all the Electors by whose suffrages the House of Commons is at present chosen.

"The popular Societies becoming so numerous, and petitioning for a Reform also becoming so general, began now to attract the notice of Government, and created an apparent alarm, which was fed and increased by the lying and interested misrepresentations of the agents of the Ministry. But the days of delusion are, I hope, passing away. The people were only claiming a restoration of those rights of which they had been at different periods unjustly and wickedly deprived by the strong hand of despotic power,—the regaining of which, by the people, would be no injury to *good* Government:—on the contrary, would prove its rightful and faithful support. But the Government appears to have thought otherwise; for, after many efforts to suppress the rising spirit of the country for a Reform of Parliament, and the persecutions, prosecutions, imprisonments, and banishments of individuals for what they termed sedition, had proved ineffectual, the Ministry at last had recourse to a still more iniquitous measure, that of charging us with HIGH TREASON. Thus the nation was deceived and stupified by alarms of plots and conspiracies that never existed, but in the wicked hearts of their fabricators. The King's Ministers, by such measures, easily effected their purpose, and a stop was put, for twenty years, to the grand cause of Parliamentary Reform. Twelve men, among the many thousands in the nation who were equally engaged in the same benevolent and patriotic cause, were now singled out as the *first* victims. This brings me to the important day which you have annually, and are at this time met to commemorate, after the lapse of *Twenty-two years.*

" The State Trials, as they are called, began, on the 25th of October, 1794, with the Trial of myself, (who was supposed to be the most helpless of this band,) which lasted nine days; and, on another memorable 5th of November, I was honourably acquitted. The then Attorney General, Sir John Scott, now Lord Eldon, took nine hours to deliver his opening Speech on that Trial. The Trial of John Horne Tooke was next in order, which lasted five days; and, on the 21st of November, he was also honourably acquitted. The Trial of John Thelwall next succeeded, which lasted three days, and he was also honourably acquitted on the 5th of December. The other prisoners, whose names were included in the same indictment, were, two days afterwards, brought to the Bar, and honourably discharged. Thus ended the momentous Trials of the year 1794. I refer you for particulars to the Trials themselves, published by Mr. Ridgway; and leave you to make your own remarks.

"I cannot help mentioning here, with sentiments of gratitude, the names of our EXCELLENT ADVOCATES *on that trying occasion*—Messrs. Erskine and Gibbs, now Lord Erskine and Judge Gibbs.

"Perhaps some of you may have a desire to be informed, how many of those twelve men, who were destined, in the councils of erring mortals, to die on a certain day, still survive. I shall only mention the names of those who have already paid the debt of nature.—The first of them who died was Thomas Holcroft; the next, John Augustus Bonney, Stewart Kyd, John Horne Tooke, Thomas Wardle, and lately, Jeremiah Joyce.

"If the recapitulation of the above circumstances shall have communicated any interesting information, or recalled to your minds any pleasing or useful recollections, it will add to the happiness of,

" DEAR SIR,

" Yours, with great respect,

"THOMAS HARDY,

" *Lately of Fleet Street.*"

" *My dear Friends and Fellow Citizens,*

"I HAVE once more the pleasure of meeting you on this Anniversary, and I thank you sincerely for your very kind and good wishes to me. I hope you will have the goodness to excuse me for reading to you a few lines, which may be thought not improper on the present occasion. The 5th of November has been a memorable day, on various accounts, in the history of England; but the 5th of November, 1794, was particularly so to me, personally. It was so, also, to some others, who are now present, and was, in a high degree, advantageous to the great cause of Freedom in this distinguished nation. Thirty-five years ago, twelve honest men gave a verdict of honourable acquittal to Thomas Hardy, who was then charged with the greatest crime known in this country—*High Treason.* After a prosecution unprecedented in the annals of this country, and a trial which lasted nine days, when the Attorney General, *Scott,* now **Lord Eldon,** made a speech, which took him nine hours to deliver, in opening the case to the Jury. This drew a very sensible remark from Lord Thurlow, at that time Chancellor. When he was informed by a messenger that the Attorney General's opening Speech occupied nine hours, he emphatically replied, ' Then by God there is no Treason!' The whole weight of the arm of power was exerted to crush me, as a prelude to the destruction of many more, which is evident from the following anecdote, well worthy of notice. It plainly appears that the Government, on the trial of Hardy, made sure of a verdict of *Guilty.* They had previously prepared eight hundred warrants, *three hundred* of which were actually signed, and some of these warrants were to have been executed that very night, and the next morning, had a different verdict been given; but who the persons thus marked out for destruction were, I did not learn: but those who informed me of that wicked design, I considered as good authority. A cloud of witnesses, and of written evidence, was brought forward against me, and a host of Crown Lawyers, such as had never before been marshalled in array against any person tried for High Treason, were employed to prove my guilt. What guilt could there be in the people associating together in a peaceable, and orderly, and legal manner, such as the *London Corresponding Society,* and other Societies, in different parts of the country, who were fairly and publicly claiming a restoration of their just rights, a more full, fair, and equal representation of the people, in the Commons' House of Parliament? There was no guilt. The guilt was on the other side, on that of despotic power, wantonly exercised by Pitt and his colleagues.

Your annually meeting, to commemorate that event, prevents it, in a great measure, from sinking into oblivion: and you will clearly observe from the anecdote I have stated, that you are not merely rejoicing yearly, for the saving of an individual, but the saving of hundreds, perhaps thousands of the greatest and best men the nation could boast of, who were devoted to an ignominious death. It is, on that account, an event worthy to be held in perpetual remembrance amongst us, as illustrative of the value of Trial by Jury—the acquittal of Hardy, Tooke, and Thelwall, on the 5th of November. In effect they were all acquitted on that day, for the charge against each was the same, and the evidence but little varied. The whole ministerial and legal phalanx were quite astounded at the first verdict; and they took eleven days to rally and recover themselves, that they might have time and strength to tutor, and sharpen their mischievous tools, before they would venture to attack a man of such distinguished talents, such a well known veteran in the cause of liberty, and one of the greatest men, perhaps, in the age which he lived, *John Horne Tooke*. His trial began on the 16th of November, and he was honourably acquitted on the 21st. After this second shameful defeat, there was another cessation of arms for ten days, to give them time to rally their discomfited, scattered, and disheartened troops, before they began their third assault, on one whom they very well knew to be a most ardent, indefatigable, and able advocate for the liberty and happiness of his fellow countrymen, and a true, and zealous promoter of a Reform in Parliament, our friend *John Thelwall*, whose trial began on the 2d of December, and who was honourably acquitted on the 5th. They were all defended by two of the most able champions the nation could produce, who vanquished the whole host of their adversaries in a triumphant manner; I mean *Erskine*, and *Gibbs*. After again resting on their arms for a few days, the other nine, who were included in the same indictment, were brought from their prisons, and our friend here, JOHN RICHTER, had the honour to be one of them, when the Attorney General, in his *great loving kindness*, called them to the bar, and discharged them without trial, not choosing to risk another disgraceful defeat. Thus ended these memorable State Trials, crowning the guilty heads of the malignant prosecutors with everlasting dishonour; after having licentiously wasted upwards of one hundred thousand pounds of the people's money, with the design to prevent that very people from demanding their just right to have *an honest Parliament.* When the Ministers had made every effort to support their false accusations of *High Treason* against those innocent men, and did not succeed, they wickedly, and impudently perverted the clearest truths, to explain away their assertions in support of the infamous doctrine of *constructive* treason; but they were completely foiled in that also, by the prompt decision of three separate, discerning, and honest juries, who pronounced the accusation a falsehood; and, in a manly way, declared, that no treason did exist. Such was the happy result of these important trials. When we look back a few years, from 1790, and forward ten or twelve years, we have but a gloomy picture to view of hundreds of our worthy fellow countrymen, who were persecuted, prosecuted, imprisoned in distant prisons, far from their families and friends, and some banished to foreign climes, for merely declaring openly, and honestly, their political principles, and opinions of the mal-administration of the Government; and suggesting, and recommending a different, more advantageous, and just administration of public affairs, which every free-born Briton is justly entitled to do. But for such patriotic conduct they were answered by the strong arm of despotic power, which visited them with total ruin, and heaped misery on their numerous and industrious families. The consequence of such cruelty, was a warm discussion of the great political question, whether this nation was really to be what it professed, and gloried in, a free country, or to be ruled by sheer despotism? The discussion became more and more animated between the friends of liberty, and the supporters of arbitrary power; and that powerful engine, the printing press, was actively employed on both sides.

The friends of liberty had nothing to fear from their opponents, for they had truth and justice decidedly with them. The force of the reasoning, and arguments of their antagonists, had little effect on the discerning public, until the Government had recourse to the argument of force; and the never failing result of all such agitation and examination, was a general diffusion of political knowledge among the people, which has been rapidly increasing to the present day. This knowledge, and spirit of inquiry, were of great use; but no thanks are due to the good intention of Ministers for having given rise to them. The Government was aware that knowledge was increasing, and that they, and their measures, were loosing ground in the public estimation. They were convinced that their severe treatment of those they had charged with libel and sedition, had a contrary effect on public opinion to what they expected, and intended it should have. Therefore, a more severe treatment still was determined on, which was no other than that *sanguinary* one which I have already noticed, trial for *High Treason*. It is worthy of remark that the Government did not succeed in taking the life of any one of the true friends of Parliamentary Reform. *Watt hypocritically professed* to be a Reformer; but on his trial it was proved that he was a Spy in the pay of Henry Dundas. He was executed at Edinburgh. Thus they hanged their own Spy for performing his business in a bungling manner, as a warning to the rest of the worthless gang. I hope you will excuse me for troubling you so long with what many of you know so well. My design in recalling these few facts to your remembrance, is chiefly for the benefit of our young friends present, some of whom were not at that period in existence. Least any of you should suppose that I have treated that Administration unfairly, although I have given you but a very short epitome of the cruel acts of the *Pitt, Dundas*, and *Grenville* system of misrule, I shall now conclude by giving you the character of that Government, freely given by *Charles James Fox*, who, you will admit, is no mean authority, in his admirable closing speech to the Electors of Westminster, on the hustings, at the contested general election, in the year 1796, when John Horne Tooke, and Admiral Gardner, were also candidates.

"Gentlemen, I have spoken plainly, and openly to you; and I will conclude with repeating that in my conscience, I believe, that the charges against the Government has been by none exaggerated. *A more detestable one never existed in British History;* and not to detain you longer, I will sum its character in a few words. *This Government has destroyed more human beings in its foreign wars, than Louis the Fourteenth; and attempted the lives of more innocent men at home, than Henry the Eighth.*"

" This was read to the company present, on Thursday, the 5th of November, 1829, at the Golden Lyon Tavern, being the 35th year after the event which they were commemorating. "THOMAS HARDY."

"FRIENDS AND FELLOW CITIZENS,

" I THANK you very kindly for your continued good wishes to me for the thirty-six years which have elapsed since that event which you are this day met here to celebrate. There are but few of our friends here present who witnessed that interesting and important event. One generation, at least, has since passed away; but we know that the beneficial consequences of that eventful period have been rapidly increasing, not only in Briton, but throughout Europe. It has led the people to think, to read, to reason, who had not before given politics a thought. Political knowledge was then generally diffused among the people, and they were informed what their rights and privileges were, and how they had been, by their governors, despoiled of them by fraud, and sometimes by force. It was a maxim of the great Lord Bacon, that *Knowledge is Power*; and we have a striking example of the truth of that maxim now before us. Since I had the happiness of meeting you in this room on the last Anniversary, there has been such an extraordinary revolution in France, that there is nothing either in antient or modern history with which it can be compared. It will, no doubt, have a beneficial effect all over Europe. I wish, with your leave, to state to you a circumstance which took place near forty years ago, about the beginning of the former French Revolution. It is this; the London Corresponding Society at that time unanimously agreed to send a Congratulatory Address to the National Convention of France, regularly and officially signed by Maurice Margarot, President, and Thomas Hardy, Secretary. The Society deputed four Members, in whom they could confide, Margarot, Hardy, Martin, and Walne, to convey it to France in the quickest and safest way they could. I called at M. Chaveline's, in Portman Square, to know whether it would be agreeable to him to convey it. He very readily agreed to it, and ordered the Deputation to wait upon him the next day at eleven. They were punctual to the time; the Address was read to him by Margarot, at which M. Chaveline was much pleased, and frankly said that he would send it very soon.

You will be so good as to observe, that M. Chaveline was sent by the National Convention of France as Ambassador to the British Government. Lord Grenville, the Foreign Secretary, and he, were sparing a little at that time, till at last all propositions from him were treated with the most sovereign contempt, and he was imperiously ordered out of the country in three days. He was treated in the same manner that Lord North and his Junta had treated Governor Penn in the beginning of the American War, when he was sent over by the Americans with a Petition to the King. The King would not see him, but contemptuously ordered him home, without condescending to receive the petition. Mark the consequence; when Governor Penn returned, the Americans declared themselves independant of this country, which has proved, no doubt, of infinite benefit to America. Of the Address to the National Convention of France, which we confided to M. Chaveline, I believe Government spies did not know; therefore, they could not report to their employers by what means that Address reached the National Convention, which was read to them, and received such high approbation. To show you that they were very highly pleased with it, they ordered it to be printed, and officially sent to all the eighty-four departments of France, and commanded it to be read at the head of all the armies. Its being the first Congratulatory Address which was sent from this country, and that too through a channel by which they could not doubt of its authenticity; namely, their own Ambassador, made it be the more taken notice of. It was published in all the French Newspapers, and afterwards copied into all the British Newspapers. Please to take notice, that this Address was presented to the French Convention before this country joined with the despots on the Continent, with the design of subjugating France, and restoring the old Government. In a most wicked and cruel Manifesto, the Duke of Brunswick at that time threatened to march to Paris, sword in hand, and rase it to the ground, and to desolate the country whereever his army should come. This roused the French, almost to a man, to oppose him. It also animated the friends of liberty in this country to address the National Convention, and promise assistance to their friends, the French, who were so laudably struggling for freedom. I shall now, with your leave, read the Address. I hope you will excuse me for being so long in introducing it. Our prosecutors considered it of great importance, for it was read three times on my trial; first, by the Attorney General; secondly, by the Solicitor General; and, finally, by the Judge. They omitted to read the last paragraph, for what reason I do not know.

" When the highly favourable reception the London Corresponding Society's Address met with was so publicly known, there followed many Addresses from this country soon after. The Society for Constitutional Information sent an Address, by their deputies, Mr. John Frost, and Mr. Joel

Barlow, which they presented to the Convention. The Society at Manchester sent an Address to the Convention, which was presented by Mr. Watt and Mr. Cooper, as their deputies, also Birmingham, Sheffield, Derby, &c. &c.

" THOMAS HARDY.

" The above observations I read to the company present, (about 150,) at the Golden Lyon Tavern, Smithfield, on Friday, the 5th of November, 1830, being the Thirty-sixth Anniversary of the acquittal of

" T. H.
30, *Queen's Row, Pimlico.*"

" DEAR SIR,

" ON the 8th of November, 1824, you was so good as to send me a folio volume *of Reports from the* SECRET *Committees of the Houses of Lords and Commons, in the months of May and June,* 1794, which you requested me to read, make my remarks on its contents, and give in *my report.* It was the first time that I had seen these Reports, although they had been printed upwards of thirty years; and although I was at that time much interested in their consequences, yet I never had the curiosity to read, or inquire further about them, especially after the very decisive opinion which twelve honest men *publicly* gave of them on *the 5th of November* of that year. On looking over the book, I saw that you had set me an arduous task, to examine such a mass of incoherent and heterogeneous materials, jumbled together with the apparent evil design to deceive and mislead the public mind, respecting the approaching trials; but fortunately for that public, they were then better informed, and had a more just and accurate knowledge of what was their political rights, privileges, and duties, than the *Secret* Committees of the Lords, and Commons expected, or *wished them to possess.* Their Reports commence with false assertions, and continue throughout with dishonest and forced constructions, and perverting the clearest truths. When these men were writing the Reports, was it possible that they could believe what they so impudently asserted? It is strange that men who are supposed to possess superior talents, education, and discernment, and who are also rulers and legislators, should suffer their evil passions to lead them, to say the least of it, into such gross errors. But what will corrupt and wicked men not do, in certain situations, to retain their assumed power, and secure to themselves the wages of iniquity? They had abundance of precedents for their base conduct, if precedent had been their plea; for there are instances sufficient, in the history of our country, of the most atrocious acts committed by imperious men, exercising usurped power, without going back for examples to *Greek* or *Roman* history. I was surprised to find, a few pages from the beginning of the volume, a display of drawings, of sergeants halberts, and spontoons, new named *battle axes, spears,* and *pikes,* which clearly appears was to give greater effect to the exhibition that was afterwards to be made to the Jury, on Hardy's Trial, of those iron instruments of human destruction. I had never seen before, either the instruments themselves, or any delineation of them, nor had I any knowledge of such things being in existence, until *Watt,* at Edinburgh, was apprehended, tried, and executed, for ordering such weapons to be manufactured. It was soon proved that *Watt* was employed as a Government spy at Edinburgh, and that they hanged their own spy for doing his business in a bungling way, as a warning to the rest of the gang. I had no knowledge of the man, nor had I any communication with him whatever; but after Watt's trial, these savage tools were brought up to London, and shown to Hardy's Jury on the trial with great pomp: and when they were one by one drawn out of the boxes, in which they were carefully arranged, and with the Attorney General's remarks on each, as they were held up to view, I remember well, that it caused a momentary shivering and horror in the crowded court and galleries, filled with ladies and gentlemen. It was done with the evident design to aggravate and heighten the effect, to blacken the character, and defame those men who were under trial, that they might, with more certainty, get a verdict against them. *The London Corresponding Society*, as a Society, never did give any countenance to the use of such instruments. Their instruments were of another and more rational kind; truth, and reason, with the copious use of the *press*, were the instruments with which the Society commenced, and which it continued to exercise, with great success. The benefits which resulted, are felt at the present day. It was very soon discovered, that several unworthy Members, who had insinuated themselves into the Society as professed Reformers, were, in reality, employed as spies, or Government reporters, as they were sometimes named; and it became notorious, that these very men were the proposers and ardent supporters of those violent and improper measures with which the Society was unfairly charged; but they were always opposed and resisted by the honest Members for Reform, who often saved the Society from being hurried *by them* into illegal and unconstitutional acts. But a small sample of the atrocity of these men was exhibited in their examination on Hardy's trial; such as Lynham, Groves, Gosling, *alias*, Douglas, Alexander, &c. and a miserable exhibition they made of it, under the searching and keen examination of the Honourable Thomas Erskine, who was well supported by Vickery Gibbs in that trial, and the trials of Tooke and Thelwall, which soon followed, all of whom were honourably acquitted. This brings to my recollection an anecdote well worthy of notice. It appears that the Government, on the trial of Hardy, made sure of a verdict of guilty; for they had prepared eight hundred warrants, *three hundred* of which were actually signed. Some of these warrants were to have been executed that very night, and the next morning, if a different verdict had been given; but who the persons were that was thus marked out for destruction, I did not learn: the gentleman who informed me of that wicked design, I considered as good authority, and I believed him. I beg to state a circumstance about the use or abuse of believing. Mr. Grant, a printer, who was a witness for the Crown, and a very useful witness he was, he being the only one the Crown could procure *not* to swear to my hand writing, but merely *to believe* it was: and it is remarkable, that the prosecutors could not prevail on one man, among all my intimate friends, who could have sworn positively to my hand writing, although they took some pains to effect it. On his first examination, the Counsel for the Crown repeatedly asked Grant, when he put letters into his hand, whether that was Hardy's hand writing, or that, or that? and he as repeatedly answered, No, that he could not take his oath that they were. Then the Counsel again and again, after he saw that he could not get him to take his oath, told him that he did not want him to swear; but he still pressed him to say that *he believed* them to be his hand writing. After some hesitation, he then said, he believed they were, but again repeated, he would not swear it; and, throughout the trial, when any of my letters or papers, with my signature, were offered to be given in evidence, and, in order to let it in, they were always handed to Grant, and he invariably said *he believed* they were, but he never swore to any of them. This *simple belief* of Grant was received by the Attorney General as evidence against a man tried for his life, on a charge of High Treason. Is that sort of testimony deemed legal, or is it customary? It appears that Grant was seized with a qualm of conscience; for I know he could not have safely sworn, having seldom had an opportunity of seeing me write, not being more than twice at my division of the Society; and even then he was at the opposite side of a broad table, where I sat to take down the name and address of any new Member, in a book for that purpose. What would have been the consequence, had he even *refused his belief*, or if such testimony had been objected to, and set aside? But no objection was made, and the trial went on.

" THOMAS HARDY."

To Mr. Place, Dec. 6, 1824.

"11*th June*, 1831.

"MY DEAR OLD FRIEND,

"I DO not desire to kill you by working you to death, but I do desire to work you pretty well, so I send you Richter's copy of the Reports of the Secret Committees, in 1794, when *murder*, under legal forms, was to have been 'the order of the day.' The notes are in Richter's hand writing, and in mine—those in my hand are correct copies of his made in pencil, copied by me lest they might be obliterated. Richter, like others, (not you,) promised me, for years, to put down on paper a number of facts respecting the London Corresponding Society; but like others, (not you,) he never performed his promise. Since his death his widow has given me the book, and you will see, from the stile of the notes, that they must have been written in gaol, before the trials in November, 1794. Now I want you to look over the book, and to write any thing, and every thing which may occur to you, and then to let me have the book again.

"I have often talked with Thelwall on the same subject, and he has sometimes promised to give me particulars; he now says he shall never find time to do so, and that unless I complete the history of the London Corresponding Society, it never will be done by any body. He and I are to meet, and to talk over particular occurrences, and he is to tell me all he can, which I am to take down; he has some memorandums and papers, which he is to look out to assist us; but 'as time flies, and man dies,' we must set to work at once, and I have sent you your task, which I hope you will attend to, as becomes a good boy.

"Your's as usual,

"FRANCIS PLACE."

To Thomas Hardy

COPY OF THOMAS HARDY'S COMMITMENT TO THE TOWER.

"THESE are, in His Majesty's name, to authorize and require you to receive into your custody the body of Thomas Hardy, herewith sent you for High Treason, and you are to keep him safe and close until he shall be delivered by due course of law; and for so doing this shall be your sufficient warrant.

"*From the Council Chamber, Whitehall, this 29th day of May, 1794.*

(Signed)

"To our very good Lord the Marquis Cornwallis, Chief Governor of His Majesty's Tower of London, or to his Deputy.

"DORSET,
MONTROSE,
SALISBURY,
CAMBDEN,
FRED. CAMPBELL,
APSLEY,
AMHERST,
AUCKLAND,
C. F. GREVILLE,
W. PITT,
HENRY DUNDAS,
THOMAS ORDE,

"D. KINGHORN, *Gentleman Gaoler, Tower of London.*"

Agreeably to the above Warrant he was delivered into the custody of the Governor of the Tower, who consigned him to the care of two Warders, whose written orders were,

"That the several persons now in the Tower, confined for High Treason, are not allowed communication with any person, without an order from His Majesty's Most Honourable Privy Council, notified to the Officer commanding in the Tower; nor is pen, ink, paper, books, or newspapers, to be permitted the prisoner without a special order.

"*Signed*, J. YORKE."

"The Warders are persons appointed to shew the armories, and other curiosities in the Tower. When on duty, their dress is like that of the Yeomen of the Guard, or Beefeaters, at St. James's. They have also the charge of persons confined for State offences, for which each Warder is allowed 17s. per week by Government.

"The Warder is not permitted to leave his prisoner by day or night, without being regularly relieved by another. To each prisoner is also appointed a soldier to guard the outside of his room, as the Warder is guardian within. Every evening the Gentleman Gaoler attends to lock up the prisoners and Warders, and he repeats his visit to open the doors, and see that all is safe, before he makes his daily report to the Governor.

"Lodging is provided for each State prisoner by the Government, at one guinea per week; and a further allowance is granted for board, according to the prisoner's rank in life. To the persons at that time confined, 13s. 4d. was regularly paid every Monday morning by the Gaoler, and a receipt taken for it in a book which he had for that purpose.

"When Mr. Burke brought in his famous Bill for reforming the Civil List, in the year 1780, among the *savings* to the nation by that bill, a mighty one was effected, by the reduction of the weekly allowance to the State prisoners in the Tower, from two guineas to 13s. 4d., which former prisoners seldom accepted, but maintained themselves; therefore the two guineas, or the 13s. 4d. went as a perquisite to the Governor. The State prisoners, in the year 1794, were informed of these circumstances, and, being rather radically inclined, considered that the 13s. 4d. would be as well in their pockets as in that of the Governor, and they all resolved to receive it.

"THOMAS HARDY."

"*Newbigging's Hotel, Lower Ryder Street,*
"*May 9th,* 1796.

" SIR,

" I AM directed by the Committee for conducting the State Trials Subscription, to transmit the following resolution to you, and to request a written answer.

" Resolved, That the Chairman be requested to ask the Defendants on what grounds they advanced certain sums to Messrs. Clarksons pending the trials, whether as complimentary fees to them, or to defray the general expences.

" I am, Sir,

" Your obedient Servant,

" WILLIAM MAXWELL."

" RECEIVED, 6th Nov. 1794, of Mr. Thomas Hardy, by the hands of Mr. George Walne, the Sum of Eighty-Three Pounds, on account of Fees and Disbursements in Mr. Hardy's late Defence, at the Suit of the King, for High Treason, for Self and Brother.

" GEORGE CLARKSON."

N. B. The Sum of Ten Pounds Ten Shillings, for the receipt of which I gave a memorandum to Mr. Walne, is included in the above.

" SIR,

" AGREEABLY to a resolution of the Committee for Conducting the State Trial Subscriptions, which I received from you, as Chairman of that Committee, I have to represent to you the following things for your consideration. Being a prisoner, I put my affairs into the hands of Mr. Walne, my brother-in-law, as an agent, (after the death of my wife,) to manage for me in the best manner he was capable of. To him, therefore, I have applied for more accurate information respecting the sum of money paid to Messrs. Clarksons at different times on my account. He has stated, fairly, I believe, in his Letter to me, for what purpose it was to be appropriated. I enclose his letter for your perusal and information. If there are any things which may not be so correctly stated as you could wish, he will readily give you, or the Committee, every information or explanation in his power that you may desire upon the subject. I have, likewise, inclosed a copy of the receipt for the £83., which receipt Mr. G. Clarkson gave me on the next day after my acquittal, when I paid him £20. of the sum.

" I am, Sir,

" Very respectfully,

" THOMAS HARDY."

To William Maxwell, Esq.
May 13, 1796.

No part of the above named subscription came into my hands, and I believe no one of the persons whom it was designed to serve got a shilling.

T. H.

The End.

www.ngramcontent.com/pod-product-compliance
Lightning Source LLC
LaVergne TN
LVHW081357060426
835510LV00016B/1886